Allyn and Bacon

Quick Guide to the Internet for for Counseling

2001 Edition

Beth Pachis

Sam Rettman

Doug Gotthoffer
California State University–Northridge

Allyn and Bacon
Boston • London • Toronto • Sydney • Tokyo • Singapore

Senior Editor: Virginia Lanigan
Multimedia Developmental Editor: Nina Tisch
Editorial Production: Marla Feuerstein
Cover Designer: Jennifer Hart
Editorial Production Service: Omegatype Typography, Inc.

NOTICE: Between the time Web site information is gathered and then published, it is not unusual for some sites to have ceased operating. Also, the transcription of URLs can result in unintended typographical errors. The Publisher would appreciate notification where these occcur so that they may be corrected in subsequent editions. Thank you.

In its effort to provide a diverse list of Web sites, the Publisher has included links that do not necessarily represent the views of Allyn and Bacon. Faculty, students, and researchers are strongly advised to use their analytical skills to determine the truth, accuracy, and value of the content in individual Web sites.

TRADEMARK CREDITS: Where information was available, trademarks and registered trademarks are indicated below. When detailed information was not available, the publisher has indicated trademark status with an initial capital where those names appear in the text.

Macintosh is a registered trademark of Apple Computer, Inc.

Microsoft is a registered trademark of Microsoft Corporation. Windows, Windows95, and Microsoft Internet Explorer are trademarks of Microsoft Corporation.

Netscape and the Netscape Navigator logo are registered trademarks of Netscape Communications Corporation.

ISBN 0-205-32391-X

Printed in the United States of America

10 9 8 7 6 5 4   03 02 01 00

Contents

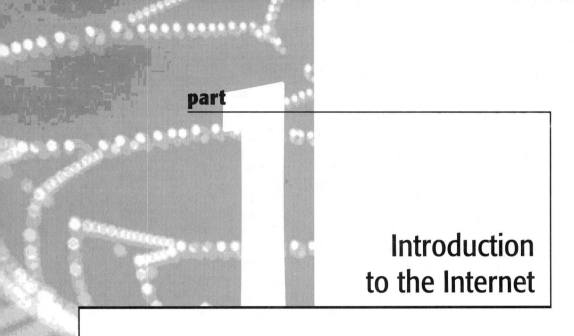

Introduction to the Internet

You're about to embark on an exciting experience as you become one of the millions of citizens of the Internet. In spite of what you might have heard, the Internet can be mastered by ordinary people before they earn a college degree and even if they're not majoring in rocket science.

Some Things You Ought to Know

Much of the confusion over the Internet comes from two sources. One is terminology. Just as the career you're preparing for has its own special vocabulary, so does the Internet. You'd be hard pressed to join in the shoptalk of archeologists, librarians, or carpenters if you didn't speak their language. Don't expect to plop yourself down in the middle of the Internet without some buzzwords under your belt, either.

The second source of confusion is that there are often many ways to accomplish the same ends on the Internet. This is a direct by-product of the freedom so highly cherished by Net citizens. When someone has an idea for doing something, he or she puts it out there and lets the Internet community decide its merits. As a result, it's difficult to put down in writing the *one exact* way to send email or find information on slugs or whatever.

In addition, there are differences in the workings of a PC or Mac and the various versions of the two major browsers, Netscape Communicator (or Navigator) and Internet Explorer. If you can't find a particular command or function mentioned in the book on your computer,

1

chances are it's there, but in a different place or with a slightly different name. Check the manual or online help that came with your computer, or ask a more computer-savvy friend or professor.

And relax. Getting up to speed on the Internet takes a little time, but the effort will be well rewarded. Approach learning your way around the Internet with the same enthusiasm and curiosity you approach learning your way around a new college campus. This isn't a competition. Nobody's keeping score. And the only winner will be you.

In *Understanding Media,* Marshall McLuhan presaged the existence of the Internet when he described electronic media as an extension of our central nervous system. On the other hand, today's students introduced to the Internet for the first time describe it as "Way cool."

No matter which description you favor, you are immersed in a period in our culture that is transforming the way we live by transforming the nature of the information we live by. As recently as 1980, intelligence was marked by "knowing things." If you were born in that year, by the time you were old enough to cross the street by yourself, that definition had changed radically. Today, in a revolution that makes McLuhan's vision tangible, events, facts, rumors, and gossip are distributed instantly to all parts of the global body. The effects are equivalent to a shot of electronic adrenaline. No longer the domain of the privileged few, information is shared by all the inhabitants of McLuhan's global village. Meanwhile, the concept of information as intelligence feels as archaic as a television remote control with a wire on it (ask your parents about that).

With hardly more effort than it takes to rub your eyes open in the morning you can connect with the latest news, with gossip about your favorite music group or TV star, with the best places to eat on spring break, with the weather back home, or with the trials and tribulations of that soap opera character whose life conflicts with your history class.

You can not only carry on a real-time conversation with your best friend at a college half a continent away, but you can see and hear her, too. Or, you can play interactive games with a dozen or more worldwide, world-class, challengers; and that's just for fun.

When it comes to your education, the Internet has shifted the focus from amassing information to putting that information to use. Newspaper and magazine archives are now almost instantly available, as are the contents of many reference books. Distant and seemingly unapproachable experts are found answering questions in discussion groups or in electronic newsletters.

The Internet also addresses the major problem facing all of us in our split-second, efficiency-rated culture: Where do we find the time? The

part

1

Internet allows professors and students to keep in touch, to collaborate and learn, without placing unreasonable demands on individual schedules. Professors are posting everything from course syllabi to homework solutions on the Internet, and are increasingly answering questions online, all in an effort to ease the pressure for face-to-face meetings by supplementing them with cyberspace offices. The Internet enables students and professors to expand office hours into a twenty-four-hour-a-day, seven-day-a-week operation. Many classes have individual sites at which enrolled students can gather electronically to swap theories, ideas, resources, gripes, and triumphs.

By freeing us from some of the more mundane operations of information gathering, and by sharpening our information-gathering skills in other areas, the Internet encourages us to be more creative and imaginative. Instead of devoting most of our time to gathering information and precious little to analyzing and synthesizing it, the Internet tips the balance in favor of the skills that separate us from silicon chips. Other Internet citizens can gain the same advantage, however, and as much as the Internet ties us together, it simultaneously emphasizes our individual skills—our ability to connect information in new, meaningful, and exciting ways. Rarely have we had the opportunity to make connections and observations on such a wide range of topics, to create more individual belief systems, and to chart a path through learning that makes information personally useful and meaningful.

part

1

A Brief History of the Internet

The 20th century's greatest advance in personal communication and freedom of expression began as a tool for national defense. In the mid-1960s, the Department of Defense was searching for an information analogy to the new Interstate Highway System, a way to move computations and computing resources around the country in the event the Cold War caught fire. The immediate predicament, however, had to do with the Defense Department's budget, and the millions of dollars spent on computer research at universities and think tanks. Much of these millions was spent on acquiring, building, or modifying large computer systems to meet the demands of the emerging fields of computer graphics, artificial intelligence, and multiprocessing (where one computer was shared among dozens of different tasks).

While the research was distributed across the country, the unwieldy, often temperamental, computers were not. This made it difficult for computer scientists at various institutions to share their computer work without duplicating each other's hardware. Wary of being accused of re-inventing the wheel, the Advanced Research Projects Agency (ARPA), the funding arm of the Defense Department, invested in the ARPANET, a private network that would allow disparate computer systems to communicate with each other. Researchers could remain ensconced among their colleagues at their home campuses while using computing resources at government research sites thousands of miles away.

A small cadre of ARPANET citizens soon began writing computer programs to perform little tasks across the Internet. Most of these programs, while ostensibly meeting immediate research needs, were written for the challenge of writing them. These programmers, for example, created the first email systems. They also created games like Space Wars and Adventure. Driven in large part by the novelty and practicality of email, businesses and institutions accepting government research funds begged and borrowed their way onto the ARPANET, and the number of connections swelled.

As the innocence of the 1960s gave way the business sense of the 1980s, the government eased out of the networking business, turning the ARPANET (now Internet) over to its users. While we capitalize the word "Internet", it may surprise you to learn there is no "Internet, Inc.," no business in charge of this uniquely postmodern creation. Administration of this world-wide communication complex is still handled by the cooperating institutions and regional networks that comprise the Internet. The word "Internet" denotes a specific interconnected network of networks, and not a corporate entity.

part

1

Using the World Wide Web for Research

Just as no one owns the worldwide communication complex that is the Internet, there is no formal organization among the collection of hundreds of thousands of computers that make up the part of the Net called the World Wide Web.

If you've never seriously used the Web, you are about to take your first steps on what can only be described as an incredible journey. Initially, though, you might find it convenient to think of the Web as a giant television network with millions of channels. It's safe to say that, among all these channels, there's something for you to watch. Only, how to find it? You could click through the channels one by one, of course, but by the time you found something of interest it would (1) be over or (2) leave you wondering if there wasn't something better on that you're missing.

A more efficient way to search for what you want would be to consult some sort of TV listing. While you could skim through pages more rapidly than channels, the task would still be daunting. A more creative approach would allow you to press a button on your remote control that would connect you to a channel of interest; what's more, that channel would contain the names (or numbers) of other channels with similar programs. Those channels in turn would contain information about other channels. Now you could zip through this million-channel universe, touching down only at programs of potential interest. This seems far more effective than the hunt-and-peck method of the traditional couch potato.

If you have a feel for how this might work for television, you have a feel for what it's like to journey around (or surf) the Web. Instead of channels on the Web, we have *Web sites*. Each site contains one or more *pages*. Each page may contain, among other things, links to other pages, either in the same site or in other sites, anywhere in the world. These other pages may elaborate on the information you're looking at or may direct you to related but not identical information, or even provide contrasting or contradictory points of view; and, of course, these pages could have links of their own.

Web sites are maintained by businesses, institutions, affinity groups, professional organizations, government departments, and ordinary people anxious to express opinions, share information, sell products, or provide services. Because these Web sites are stored electronically, updating them is more convenient and practical than updating printed media. That makes Web sites far more dynamic than other types of research material you may be used to, and it means a visit to a Web site can open up new opportunities that weren't available as recently as a few hours ago.

part

1

Hypertext and Links

The invention that unveils these revolutionary possibilities is called *hypertext*. Hypertext is a technology for combining text, graphics, sounds, video, and links on a single World Wide Web page. Click on a link and you're transported, like Alice falling down the rabbit hole, to a new page, a new address, a new environment for research and communication.

Links come in three flavors: text, picture, and hot spot. A text link may be a letter, a word, a phrase, a sentence, or any contiguous combination of text characters. You can identify text links at a glance because the characters are <u>underlined</u>, and are often displayed in a unique color, setting the link apart from the rest of the text on the page. Picture links

Text
Link

Picture
Link

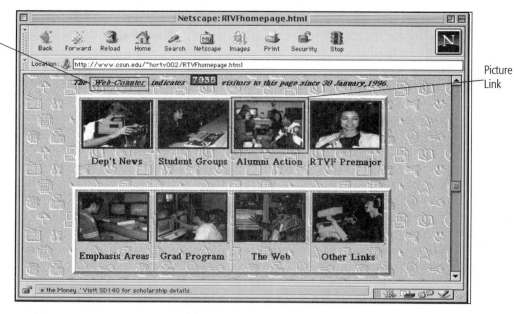

Text links are underlined and set of in color. Picture links are set off by a colored border. Hot spots carry no visual identification.

are pictures or other graphic elements. On the Web, a picture may not only be worth a thousand words, but it may also be the start of a journey into a whole new corner of cyberspace.

The third kind of link, the hot spot, is neither underlined nor bordered, a combination which would make it impossible to spot, were it not for a Web convention that offers you a helping hand finding all types of links. This helping hand is, well, a hand. Whenever the mouse cursor passes over a link, the cursor changes from an arrow to a hand. Wherever you see the hand icon, you can click and retrieve another Web page. Sweep the cursor over an area of interest, see the hand, follow the link, and you're surfing the Web.

In the Name of the Page

Zipping around the Web in this way may seem exciting, even serendipitous, but it's also fraught with perils. How, for instance, do you revisit a page of particular interest? Or share a page with a classmate? Or cite a page as a reference for a professor? Web page designers assign names, or titles, to their pages; unfortunately, there's nothing to prevent two designers from assigning the same title to different pages.

An instrument that uniquely identifies Web pages does exist. It's called a Universal Resource Locator (URL), the cyber-signposts of the World Wide Web. URLs contain all the information necessary to locate:

- the page containing the information you're looking for;
- the computer that hosts (stores) that page of information;
- the form the information is stored in.

A typical URL looks like this:

```
http://www.abacon.com/index.html
```

You enter it into the **Location** or **Address** field at the top of your browser window. Hit the **Return** (or **Enter**) key and your browser will deliver to your screen the exact page specified. When you click on a link, you're actually using a shorthand alternative to typing the URL yourself because the browser does it for you. In fact, if you watch the "Location" or "Address" field when you click on a link, you'll see its contents change to the URL you're traveling to.

part

1

The URL Exposed

How does your browser—or the whole World Wide Web structure, for that matter—know where you're going? As arcane as the URL appears, there is a logical explanation to its apparent madness. (This is true not only of URLs but also of your computer experience in general. Because a computer's "intelligence" only extends to following simple instructions exactly, most of the commands, instructions, and procedures you'll encounter have simple underlying patterns. Once you familiarize yourself with these patterns, you'll find you're able to make major leaps in your understanding of new Internet features.)

To unscramble the mysteries of World Wide Web addresses, we'll start at the end of the URL and work our way toward the front.

```
/index.html
```

This is the name of a single file or document. Eventually, the contents of this file/document will be transferred over the Internet to your computer.

However, because there are undoubtedly thousands of files on the Internet with this name, we need to clarify our intentions a bit more.

```
www.abacon.com
```

This is the name of a particular Internet *Web server,* a computer whose job it is to forward Web pages to you on request. By Internet convention, this name is unique. The combination of

```
www.abacon.com/index.html
```

identifies a unique file/document on a unique Web server on the World Wide Web. No other file has this combined address, so there's no question about which file/document to transfer to you.

The characters *http://* at the beginning of the URL identify the method by which the file/document will be transferred. The letters stand for **HyperText Transfer Protocol.**

Quick Check

Don't Be Lost In (Hyper)Space

Let's pause for a quick check of your Web navigation skills. Look at the sample web page on the next page. How many links does it contain?

Did you find all five? That's right, five:

■ The word "links" in the second line below the seaside picture;

■ The sentence "What about me?";

■ The word "cyberspace" in the quick brown fox sentence;

■ The red and white graphic in the lower left-hand corner of the page. The blue border around it matches the blue of the text links;

■ The hot spot in the seaside picture. We know there's at least one link in the picture, because the cursor appears as a hand. (There may be more hot spots on the page, but we can't tell from this picture alone.)

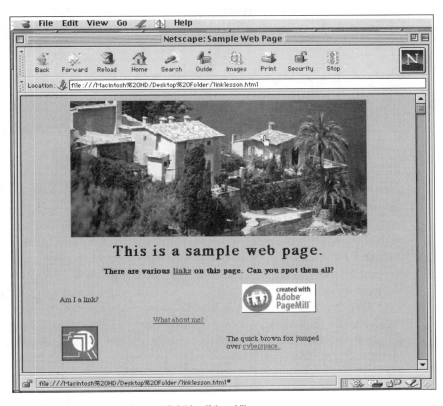

A sample web page to exercise your link identifying skills.

Getting There from Here

Now you know that a URL uniquely identifies a page and that links used as shorthand for URLs enable you to travel from page to page in the Web; but what if a link takes you someplace you don't want to go? Missing page messages take several forms, such as URL 404, Object not on this server, Missing Object, Page not Found, but they all lead to the same place—a dead end. The page specified by the link or URL no longer exists. There are many reasons for missing pages. You may have entered the URL incorrectly. Every character must be precise and no spaces are allowed. More than likely, though, especially if you arrived here via a link, the page you're after has been moved or removed. Remember, anybody can create a link to any page. In the spirit of the Internet, there are no forms to fill out, no procedures to follow. That's the good news. The bad news is that the owner of a page is under no

part

1

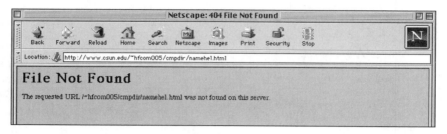

A missing page message, an all too common road hazard on the information superhighway.

obligation to inform the owners of links pointing to it that the page location has changed. In fact, there's no way for the page owner to even know about all the links to her page. Yes, the Internet's spirit of independence proves frustrating sometimes, but you'll find these small inconveniences are a cheap price to pay for the benefits you receive. Philosophy aside, though, we're still stuck on a page of no interest to us. The best strategy is to back up and try another approach.

Every time you click on the **Back** button, you return to the previous page you visited. That's because your browser keeps track of the pages you visit and the order in which you visit them. The **Back** icon, and its counterpart, the **Forward** icon, allow you to retrace the steps, forward and backward, of your cyberpath. Sometimes you may want to move two, three, or a dozen pages at once. Although you can click the **Back** or **Forward** icons multiple times, Web browsers offer an easier navigation shortcut. If you use Netscape, clicking on the **Go** menu in the menu bar displays a list of your most recently visited pages, in the order you've been there. Unlike the **Back** or **Forward** icons, you can select any page from the menu, and a single click takes you directly there. There's no need to laboriously move one page a time. If you use Internet Explorer, you can click on the **History** button in the Explorer bar to see a list of links you visited in previous days and weeks, or press the arrow at the end of the Address bar to see previously visited links.

Quick Check

As a quick review, here's what we know about navigating the Web so far:

- Enter a URL directly into the Location field;
- Click on a link;
- Use the **Back** or **Forward** icons;
- Select a page from the **Go** menu.

You Can Go Home (and to Other Pages) Again

How do we return to a page hours, days, or even months later? One way is to write down the URLs of every page we may want to revisit. There's got to be a better way, and there is: We call them bookmarks (on Netscape Communicator) or favorites (on Microsoft Internet Explorer).

Like their print book namesakes, Web bookmarks (and favorites) flag specific Web pages. Selecting an item from the **Bookmark/Favorites** menu, like selecting an item from the **Go** menu, is the equivalent of entering a URL into the **Location** field of your browser, except that items in the **Bookmark/Favorites** menu are ones you've added yourself and represent pages visited over many surfing experiences, not just the most recent one.

To select a page from your bookmark list, pull down the **Bookmark/Favorites** menu and click on the desired entry. To save a favorite page location, use the Add feature available in both browsers. In Netscape Communicator, clicking on the **Add Bookmark** command makes a bookmark entry for the current page. **Add to Favorites** performs the same function in Microsoft Internet Explorer. Clicking this feature adds the location of the current page to your **Bookmark/Favorites** menu.

part

1

A cautionary note is in order here. Your bookmark or favorites list physically exists only on your personal computer, which means that if you connect to the Internet on a different computer, your list won't be available. If you routinely connect to the Internet from a computer lab, for example, get ready to carry the URLs for your favorite Web sites in your notebook or your head.

Searching and Search Engines

Returning to our cable television analogy, you may recall that we conveniently glossed over the question of how we selected a starting channel in the first place. With a million TV channels, or several million Web pages, we can't depend solely on luck guiding us to something interesting.

On the Web, we solve the problem with specialized computer programs called *search engines* that crawl through the Web, page by page, cataloging its contents. As different software designers developed search strategies, entrepreneurs established Web sites where any user could find pages containing particular words and phrases. Today, Web sites such as Yahoo!, AltaVista, Excite, WebCrawler, and HotBot offer you a "front door" to the Internet that begins with a search for content of interest.

The URLs for some popular search sites are:

Excite	`www.excite.com`
Yahoo!	`www.yahoo.com`
AltaVista	`www.altavista.digital.com`
WebCrawler	`www.webcrawler.com`
MetaCrawler	`www.metacrawler.com`
Infoseek	`www.infoseek.com`
HotBot	`www.hotbot.com`

Internet Gold Is Where You Find It

Let's perform a simple search using HotBot to find information about the history of the Internet.

part

1

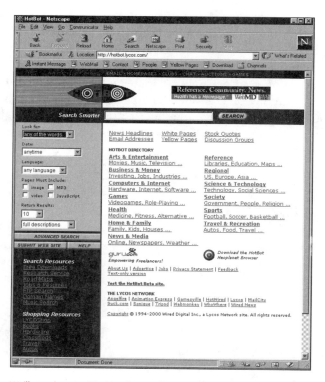

We'll start by searching for the words "internet" or "history." By looking for "any of the words," the search will return pages on which either "internet" or "history" or both appear.

Our search returned more than 1,000,000 matches or *hits.* Pages are ranked according to the following factors: words in the title, keyword meta tags, word frequency in the document, and document length.

We can conduct the same search, but this time look for "all the words." The search will return hits when both "internet" and "history" appear on the same page, in any order, and not necessarily next to each other.

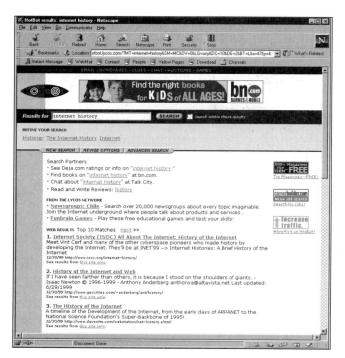

The search is narrowed down somewhat, but still has more than 1,000,000 hits.

part

1

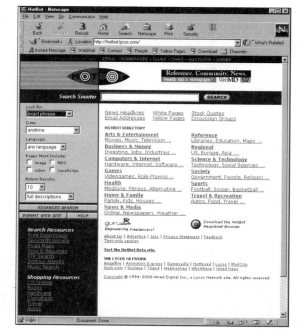

When we search for the exact phrase "internet history," which means those two words in exactly that order, with no intervening words, we're down to several thousand hits (still a substantial number).

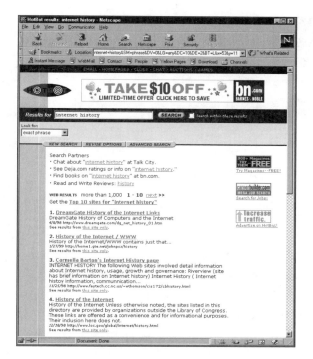

Now the first hits may be more specific. However, other hits in the list may have nothing to do with the history of the Internet. Hits happen. No search engine is 100 percent accurate 100 percent of the time. Spurious search results are the serendipity of the Internet. Look at them as an opportunity to explore something new.

Out of curiosity, let's try our history of the Internet search using a different search engine. When we search for the phrase "history of the internet" using WebCrawler, the quotation marks serve the same purpose as selecting "the exact phrase" option in Hotbot. The WebCrawler search only finds a few hundred hits. Some are the same as those found using HotBot, some are different. Different searching strategies and software algorithms make using more than one search engine a must for serious researchers.

The major search engines conveniently provide you with tips to help you get the most out of their searches. These include ways to use AND and OR to narrow down searches, and ways to use NOT to eliminate unwanted hits.

Each search engine also uses a slightly different approach to cataloging the Web, so at different sites your results might vary. Often, one search engine provides better results (more relevant hits) in your areas of interest; sometimes, the wise strategy is to provide the same input to several different engines. No one search engine does a perfect job all the time, so experience will dictate the one that's most valuable for you.

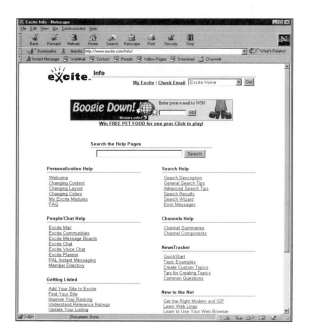

You'll find search tip pages like this at all the major search engine sites.

Quick Check

Let's review our searching strategies:

- Visit one of the search engine sites;
- Enter key words or phrases that best describe the search criteria;
- Narrow the search if necessary by using options such as "all the words" or "the exact phrase." On some search engines, you may use the word "and" or the symbol "|" to indicate words that all must appear on a page;
- Try using the same criteria with different search engines.

How Not to Come Down with a Virus

Downloading files from the Internet allows less responsible Net citizens to unleash onto your computer viruses, worms, and Trojan horses, all dangerous programs that fool you into thinking they're doing one thing while they're actually erasing your hard disk or performing some other undesirable task. Protection is your responsibility.

One way to reduce the risk of contracting a virus is to download software from reliable sites. Corporations such as Microsoft and Apple take care to make sure downloadable software is virus free. So do most institutions that provide software downloads as a public service (such as the Stanford University archives of Macintosh software). Be especially careful of programs you find on someone's home page. If you're not sure about safe download sources, ask around in a newsgroup (discussed shortly), talk to friends, or check with the information technology center on campus.

You can also buy and use a reliable virus program. Norton, Symantec, and Dr. Solomon all sell first-rate programs for the Mac and PC. You can update these programs right from the Internet so they'll detect the most current viruses. Most of the time, these programs can disinfect files/documents on your disk that contain viruses. Crude as it may sound, downloading programs from the Internet without using a virus check is like having unprotected sex with a stranger. While downloading software may not be life threatening, imagine the consequences if your entire hard disk, including all your course work and software, is totally obliterated. It won't leave you feeling very good.

part

1

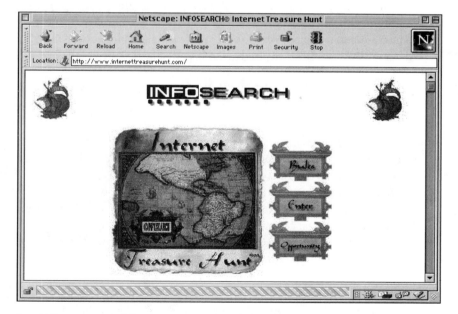

If you'd like some entertaining practice sharpening your Web searching skills, point your browser to <www.internettreasurehunt.com>, follow the directions, and you're on your way to becoming an Internet researcher extraordinaire.

The (E)mail Goes Through

Email was one of the first applications created for the Internet by its designers, who sought a method of communicating with each other directly from their keyboards. Your electronic Internet mailbox is to email what a post office box is to "snail mail" (the name Net citizens apply to ordinary, hand-delivered mail). This mailbox resides on the computer of your Internet Service Provider (ISP). That's the organization providing you with your Internet account. Most of the time your ISP will be your school; but, you may contract with one of the commercial providers, such as America Online, Mindspring, Microsoft Network, Earthlink, or AT&T. The Internet doesn't deliver a message to your door but instead leaves it in a conveniently accessible place (your mailbox) in the post office (the computer of your ISP), until you retrieve the mail using your combination (password).

part

1

If you currently have computer access to the Internet, your school or ISP assigned you a *user name* (also called a user id, account name, or account number). This user name may be your first name, your first initial and the first few characters of your last name, or some strange combination of numbers and letters only a computer could love. An email address is a combination of your user name and the unique address of the computer through which you access your email, like this:

    username@computername.edu

The three letters after the dot, in this case "edu," identify the top level "domain." There are six common domain categories in use: edu (educational), com (commercial), org (organization), net (network), mil (military), and gov (government). The symbol "@"—called the "at" sign in typewriter days—serves two purposes: For computers, it provides a neat, clean separation between your user name and the computer name; for people, it makes Internet addresses more pronounceable. Your address is read: user name "at" computer name "dot" e-d-u. Suppose your Internet user name is "a4736g" and your ISP is Allyn & Bacon, the publisher of this book. Your email address might look like

    a4736g@abacon.com

and you would tell people your email address is "ay-four-seven-three-six-gee at ay bacon dot com."

We Don't Just Handle Your Email, We're Also a Client

You use email with the aid of special programs called *mail clients*. As with search engines, mail clients have the same set of core features, but your access to these features varies with the type of program. On both the PC and the Mac, Netscape Communicator and Microsoft Internet Explorer give you access to mail clients while you're plugged into the Web. That way you can pick up and send mail while you're surfing the Web.

The basic email service functions are creating and sending mail, reading mail, replying to mail, and forwarding mail. First we'll examine the process of sending and reading mail, and then we'll discuss how to set up your programs so that your messages arrive safely.

Let's look at a typical mail client screen, in this case from Netscape Communicator 4.7. You reach this screen by choosing **Messenger** from under the **Communicator** menu. To send a message from scratch, choose the **New Msg** button to create a blank message form, which has fields for the recipient's address and the subject, and a window for the text of the message.

Fill in the recipient's address in the "To" field, just above the arrow. Use your own address. We'll send email to ourselves and use the same

part

1

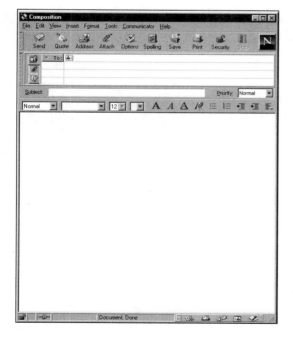

New message form, with fields for recipient's address and the subject, and a window for the text of the message.

message to practice sending email and reading it as well; then we'll know if your messages come out as expected.

Click in the "Subject" field and enter a word or phrase that generally describes the topic of the message. Since we're doing this for the first time, let's type "Maiden Email Voyage."

Now click anywhere in the text window and enter your message. Let's say "Hi. Thanks for guiding me through sending my first email." You'll find that the mail client works here like a word processing program, which means you can insert and delete words and characters and highlight text.

Now click the **Send** button on the Navigation toolbar. You've just created and sent your first email message. In most systems, it takes a few seconds to a few minutes for a message to yourself to reach your mailbox, so you might want to take a short break before continuing. When you're ready to proceed, close the **Composition** window and click the **Get Msg** button.

What Goes Around Comes Around

part
1

Now let's grab hold of the message you just sent to yourself. When retrieving mail, most mail clients display a window showing the messages in your mailbox telling you how many new messages have been added.

If you've never used your email before, chances are your message window is empty, or contains only one or two messages (usually official messages from the ISP) besides the one you sent to yourself. The message to yourself should be accompanied by an indicator of some sort—a colored mark, the letter N—indicating it's a new message. In Netscape Communicator, as in other mail clients, you also get to see the date of the message, who sent it, and the information you entered in the subject line. The Subject field lets you scan your messages and determine which ones you want to look at first.

The summary of received messages tells you everything you need to know about a message except what's in it. Click anywhere in the line to see the contents in the message window. Click on the message from yourself and you'll see the contents of the message displayed in a window. The information at the top—To, From, Subject, and so forth—is called the *header*. Depending on your system, you may also see some cryptic lines with terms such as X-Mailer, received by, and id number. Most of the time, there's nothing in this part of the header of interest, so just skip over it for now.

Moving Forward

The contents, or text, of your message can be cut and pasted just like any other text document. If you and a classmate are working on a project together, your partner can write part of a paper and email it to you, and you can copy the text from your email message and paste it into your word processing program.

What if there are three partners in this project? One partner sends you a draft of the paper for you to review. You like it and want to send it on to your other partner. The **Forward** feature lets you send the message intact, so you don't have to cut and paste it into a new message window. To forward a message, highlight it in the **Inbox** (top) and click the **Forward** icon. Enter the recipient's address in the "To" field of the message window. Note that the subject of the message is "Fwd:" followed by the subject of the original message. Use the text window to add your comments ahead of the original message.

A Chance to Reply

Email is not a one-way message system. Let's walk through a reply to a message from a correspondent named Elliot. Highlight the message in your **Inbox** again and this time click on the **Reply** icon. Depending on which program you're using, you'll see that each line in the message is preceded by either a vertical bar or a right angle bracket (>).

Note the "To" and "Subject" fields are filled in automatically with the address of the sender and the original subject preceded by "Re:". In Internet terminology, the message has been *quoted*. The vertical bar or > is used to indicate lines not written by you but by someone else (in this case, the message's original author). Why bother? Because this feature allows you to reply without retyping the parts of the message you're responding to. Because your typing isn't quoted, your answers stand out from the original message. Netscape Communicator 4.7 adds some blank lines above and below your comments, a good practice for you if your mail client doesn't do this automatically.

Welcome to the Internet, Miss Manners

While we're on the subject of email, here are some *netiquette* (net etiquette) tips.

part

1

- When you send email to someone, even someone who knows you well, all they have to look at are your words—there's no body language attached. That means there's no smile, no twinkle in the eye, no raised eyebrow; and especially, there's no tone of voice. What you write is open to interpretation and your recipient has nothing to guide him or her. You may understand the context of a remark, but will your reader? If you have any doubts about how your message will be interpreted, you might want to tack on an *emoticon* to your message. An emoticon is a face created out of keyboard characters. For example, there's the happy Smiley :-) (you have to look at it sideways . . . the parenthesis is its mouth), the frowning Smiley :-((Frownie?), the winking Smiley ;-), and so forth. Smileys are the body language of the Internet. Use them to put remarks in context. "Great," in response to a friend's suggestion means you like the idea. "Great :-(" changes the meaning to one of disappointment or sarcasm. (Want a complete list of emoticons? Try using "emoticon" as a key word for a Web search.)

- Keep email messages on target. One of the benefits of email is its speed. Reading through lengthy messages leaves the reader wondering when you'll get to the point.

- Email's speed carries with it a certain responsibility. Its ease of use and the way a messages seems to cry out for an answer both encourage quick responses, but quick doesn't necessarily mean thoughtful. Once you hit the **Send** icon, that message is gone. There's no recall button. Think before you write, lest you feel the wrath of the modern-day version of your parents' adage: Answer in haste, repent at leisure.

Keeping Things to Yourself

Here's another tip cum cautionary note, this one about Web security. Just as you take care to protect your wallet or purse while walking down a crowded street, it's only good practice to exercise caution with information you'd like to keep (relatively) private. Information you pass around the Internet is stored on, or passed along by, computers that are accessible to others. Although computer system administrators take great care to insure the security of this information, no scheme is completely infallible. Here are some security tips:

- Exercise care when sending sensitive information such as credit card numbers, passwords, even telephone numbers and addresses in plain email. Your email message may pass through four or five computers en route to its destination, and at any of these points, it can be intercepted and read by someone other than the recipient.

- Send personal information over the Web only if the page is secure. Web browsers automatically encrypt information on secure pages, and the information can only be unscrambled at the Web site that created the secure page. You can tell if a page is secure by checking the status bar at the bottom of your browser's window for an icon of a closed lock.

- Remember that any files you store on your ISP's computer are accessible to unscrupulous hackers.

- Protect your password. Many Web client programs, such as mail clients, have your password for you. That means anyone with physical access to your computer can read your email. With a few simple tools, someone can even steal your password. Never leave your password on a lab computer. (Make sure the **Remember Password** or **Save Password** box is unchecked in any application that asks for your password.)

part

1

The closed lock icon in the lower left-hand corner of your browser window indicates a "secure" Web page.

An Audience Far Wider Than You Imagine

Remember that the Web in particular and the Internet in general are communications mediums with a far-reaching audience, and placing information on the Internet is tantamount to publishing it. Certainly, the contents of any message or page you post become public information, but in a newsgroup (an electronic bulletin board), your email address also becomes public knowledge. On a Web page, posting a photo of your favorite music group can violate the photographer's copyright, just as if you published the image in a magazine. Use common sense about posting information you or someone else expects to remain private; and, remember, information on the Web can and will be read by people with different tastes and sensitivities. The Web tends to be self-censoring, so be prepared to handle feedback, both good and bad.

A Discussion of Lists

There's no reason you can't use email to create a discussion group. You pose a question, for example, by sending an email message to everyone in the group. Somebody answers and sends the answer to everyone else on the list, and so on.

At least, that's the theory.

In practice, this is what often happens. As people join and leave the group, you and the rest of your group are consumed with updating your lists, adding new names and deleting old ones. As new people join, their addresses may not make it onto the lists of all the members of the group, so different participants get different messages. The work of administering the lists becomes worse than any value anyone can get out of the group, and so it quickly dissolves.

Generally, you're better off letting the computer handle discussion group administration. A *list server* is a program for administering emailing lists. It automatically adds and deletes list members and handles the distribution of messages.

Tile.Net offfers shortcuts to working your way through the Internet's maze of discussion lists.

Thousands of mailing lists have already been formed by users with common interests. You may find mailing lists for celebrities, organizations, political interests, occupations, and hobbies. Your instructor may establish a mailing list for your course.

Groups come in several different flavors. Some are extremely active. You can receive as many as forty or more email messages a day. Other lists may send you a message a month. One-way lists, such as printed newsletters, do not distribute your reply to any other subscriber. Some lists distribute replies to everyone. These lists include mediated lists, in which an "editor" reviews each reply for suitability (relevance, tone, use of language) before distributing the message, and unmediated lists, in which each subscriber's response is automatically distributed to all the other subscribers with no restrictions except those dictated by decency and common sense, though these qualities may not always be obvious from reading the messages.

Get on a List Online

You join in the discussion by subscribing to a list, which is as straightforward as sending email. You need to know only two items: the name of the list and the address of the list server program handling subscriptions. To join a list, send a **Subscribe** message to the list server address. The message is usually as simple as "subscribe," the name of the list, and your name (your real name, not your user name), all on one line. *And that's all.* This message will be read by a computer program that looks for these items only. At the very best, other comments in the message will be ignored. At the very worst, your entire message will be ignored, and so will you.

Within a few hours to a day after subscribing, the list server will automatically send you a confirmation email message, including instructions for sending messages, finding out information about the list and its members, and canceling your subscription. Save this message for future reference. That way, if you do decide to leave the list, you won't have to circulate a message to the members asking how to unsubscribe, and you won't have to wade through fifty replies all relaying the same information you received when you joined.

Soon after your confirmation message appears in your mailbox, and depending on the activity level of the list, you'll begin receiving email messages. New list subscribers customarily wait a while before joining the discussion. After all, you're electronically strolling into a room full of strangers; it's only fair to see what topics are being discussed before

part

1

wading in with your own opinions. Otherwise, you're like the bore at the party who elbows his way into a conversation with "But enough about you, let's talk about me." You'll also want to avoid the faux pas of posting a long missive on a topic that subscribers spent the preceding three weeks thrashing out. Observe the list for a while, understand its tone and feel, what topics are of interest to others and what areas are taboo. Also, look for personalities. Who's the most vociferous? Who writes very little but responds thoughtfully? Who's the most flexible? The most rigid? Most of all, keep in mind that there are far more observers than participants. What you write may be read by 10 or 100 times more people than those whose names show up in the daily messages.

When you reply to a message, you reply to the list server address, not to the address of the sender (unless you intend for your communication to remain private). The list server program takes care of distributing your message listwide. Use the address in the "Reply To" field of the message. Most mail clients automatically use this address when you select the **Reply** command. Some may ask if you want to use the reply address (say yes). Some lists will send a copy of your reply to you so you know your message is online. Others don't send the author a copy, relying on your faith in the infallibility of computers.

In the words of those famous late night television commercials, you can cancel your subscription at any time. Simply send a message to the address you used to subscribe (which you'll find on that confirmation message you saved for reference), with "unsubscribe," followed on the same line by the name of the list. For example, to leave a list named "WRITER-L," you would send:

```
unsubscribe WRITER-L
```

Even if you receive messages for a short while afterwards, have faith— they will disappear.

Waste Not, Want Not

List servers create an excellent forum for people with common interests to share their views; however, from the Internet standpoint, these lists are terribly wasteful. First of all, if there are one thousand subscribers to a list, every message must be copied one thousand times and distributed over the Internet. If there are forty replies a day, this one list creates forty thousand email messages. Ten such lists mean almost a half million messages, most of which are identical, flying around the Net.

Another wasteful aspect of list servers is the way in which messages are answered. The messages in your mailbox on any given day represent a combination of new topics and responses to previous messages. But where are these previous messages? If you saved them, they're in your email mailbox taking up disk space. If you haven't saved them, you have nothing to compare the response to. What if a particular message touches off a chain of responses, with subscribers referring not only to the source message but to responses as well? It sounds like the only safe strategy is to save every message from the list, a suggestion as absurd as it is impractical.

What we really need is something closer to a bulletin board than a mailing list. On a bulletin board, messages are posted once. Similar notices wind up clustered together. Everyone comes to the same place to read or post messages.

And Now the News(group)

The Internet equivalent of the bulletin board is the Usenet or newsgroup area. Usenet messages are copied only once for each ISP supporting the newsgroup. If there are one thousand students on your campus reading the same newsgroup message, there need only be one copy of the message stored on your school's computer.

Categorizing a World of Information

Newsgroups are categorized by topics, with topics broken down into subtopics and sub-subtopics. For example, you'll find newsgroups devoted to computers, hobbies, science, social issues, and "alternatives." Newsgroups in this last category cover a wide range of topics that may not appeal to the mainstream. Also in this category are beginning newsgroups.

Usenet names are amalgams of their topics and subtopics, separated by dots. If you were interested in a newsgroup dealing with, say, music, you might start with rec.music and move down to rec.music.radiohead, or rec.music.techno, and so forth. The naming scheme allows you to zero in on a topic of interest.

Getting into the News(group) Business

Most of the work of reading, responding to, and posting messages is handled by a news reader client program, accessible through both Netscape Communicator and Microsoft Internet Explorer. You can not only surf the Web and handle your mail via your browser, but you can also drop into your favorite newsgroups virtually all in one operation.

Let's drop into a newsgroup. To reach groups via Netscape Communicator 4.7, go to the Communicator menu bar and select **Newsgroups.** Then, from the File menu, select **Subscribe.** A dialogue box will open that displays a list of available groups.

To subscribe to a newsgroup—that is, to tell your news reader you want to be kept up-to-date on the messages posted to a particular group—highlight the group of interest and click on **Subscribe.** Alternately, you can click in the Subscribe column to the right of the group name. The check mark in the Subscribe column means you're "in." Now, click **OK.**

part 1

The message center in Netscape Communicator displays a list of newsgroups on your subscription list. Double click on the one of current interest and your reader presents you with a list of messages posted on the group's bulletin board. Double click on a message to open its contents in a window.

Often, messages contain "Re:" in their subject lines, indicating a response to a previous message (the letters stand for "Regarding"). Many news readers maintain a *thread* for you. Threads are chains of messages and all responses to that message. These readers give you the option to read messages chronologically or to read a message followed by its responses.

When you subscribe to a newsgroup, your news reader will also keep track of the messages you've read so that it can present you with the newest (unread) ones. While older messages are still available to you, this feature guarantees that you stay up-to-date without any record keeping on your part. Subscribing to a newsgroup is free, and the subscription information resides on your computer.

Newsgroups have no way of knowing who their subscribers are, and the same caveat that applies to bookmarks applies to newsgroups. Information about your subscriptions resides physically on the personal computer you're using. If you switch computers, as in a lab, your subscription information and history of read messages are beyond your reach.

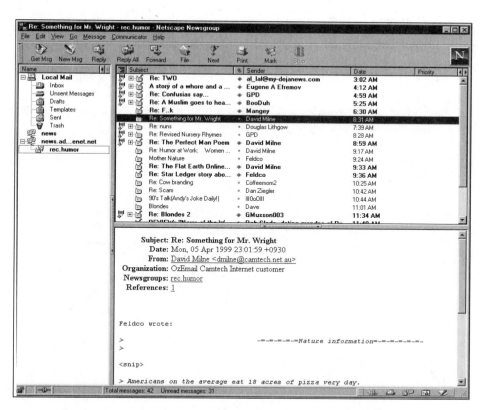

The top part of this figure shows a listing of posted messages. While not visible from this black and white reproduction, a red indicator in the Subject column marks unread messages. Double-clicking on a message opens its contents into a window shown in the bottom part of this figure. You can reply to this message via the Reply icon, or get the next message using the Next icon.

part

1

Welcome to the Internet, Miss Manners—Again

As with list servers, hang out for a while, or *lurk,* to familiarize yourself with the style, tone, and content of newsgroup messages. As you probably surmised from the names of the groups, their topics of discussion are quite narrow. One of the no-nos of newsgroups is posting messages on subjects outside the focus of the group. Posting off-topic messages, especially lengthy ones, is an excellent way to attract a flaming.

A *flame* is a brutally debasing message from one user to another. Flames are designed to hurt and offend, and often the target of the flame feels compelled to respond in kind to protect his or her self-esteem. This leads to a *flame war,* as other users take sides and wade in with flames of their own. If you find yourself the target of a flame, your best strategy is to ignore it. As with a campfire, if no one tends to the flames, they soon die out.

As mentioned earlier, posting messages to newsgroups is a modern form of publishing, and a publisher assumes certain responsibilities. You have a duty to keep your messages short and to the point. Many newsgroup visitors connect to the Internet via modems. Downloading a day's worth of long postings, especially uninteresting ones, is annoying and frustrating. Similarly, don't post the same message to multiple, re-lated newsgroups. This is called *cross posting,* and it's a peeve of Net citizens who check into these groups. If you've ever flipped the television from channel to channel during a commercial break only to encounter the same commercial (an advertising practice called *roadblocking*), you can imagine how annoying it is to drop in on several newsgroups only to find the same messages posted to each one.

With the huge potential audience newsgroups offer, you might think you've found an excellent medium for advertising goods or services. After all, posting a few messages appears analogous to running classified ads in newspapers, only here the cost is free. There's a name for these kinds of messages—*spam.* Spam is the junk mail of the Internet, and the practice of spamming is a surefire way to attract flames. The best advice for handling spam? Don't answer it. Not only does an answer encourage the spammer, but he or she will also undoubtedly put your email address on a list and sell it to other spammers, who will flood your online mail-box with their junk.

Above all, be considerate of others. Treat them the way you'd like to be treated. Do you enjoy having your grammar or word choices cor-rected in front of the whole world? Do you feel comfortable when some-one calls you stupid in public? Do you appreciate having your religion, ethnicity, heritage, or gender belittled in front of an audience? Respect the rights and feelings of others, if not out of simple decency then out of the sanctions your ISP may impose. Although you have every right to ex-press an unpopular opinion or to take issue with the postings of others, most ISPs have regulations about the kinds of messages one can send via their facilities. Obscenities, threats, and spam may, at a minimum, result in your losing your Internet access privileges.

part

1

Give Your Web Browser Some Personality—Yours

Before accessing email and newsgroup functions, you need to set up or personalize your browser. If you always work on the same personal computer, this is a one-time operation that takes only a few minutes. In it, you tell your browser where to find essential computer servers, along with personal information the Internet needs to move messages for you.

- *Step 1:* Open the **Preferences** menu in Netscape or the **Internet Options** in Internet Explorer. In Netscape Communicator the Preferences menu is located under the **Edit** menu; in Microsoft Internet Explorer the Internet Options can be found under the **View** menu.

- *Step 2:* Tell the browser who you are and where to find your mail servers. Your Reply To address is typically the same as your email address, though if you have an email alias you can use it here. Your ISP will provide the server names and addresses. SMTP handles your outgoing messages, while the POP3 server routes incoming mail. Often, but not always, these server names are the same.

- *Step 3:* Tell the browser where to find your news server. Your ISP will furnish the name of the server. Note that in Microsoft Internet Explorer, you specify a helper application to read the news. Now that most computers come with browsers already loaded onto the hard disk, you'll find that these helper applications are already set up for you.

- *Step 4:* Set your home page. For convenience, you may want your browser to start by fetching a particular page, such as your favorite search site. Or you might want to begin at your school library's home page. Enter the URL for this starting page in the home page address field. Both Netscape and Microsoft offer the option of no home page when you start up. In that case, you get a blank browser window.

part

1

Operating systems such as Mac OS 8 and Microsoft Windows 95 and 98 offer automated help in setting up your browsers for Web, mail, and newsgroup operation. You need to know the names of the servers mentioned above, along with your user name and other details, such as the address of the domain name server (DNS) of your ISP. You should receive all this information when you open your Internet account. If not, ask for it.

Navigating the Internet

FTP

FTP allows Internet users to transfer files from one computer to another, no matter where in the world the computers are located. Information of all kinds—reports, guides, books, statistical tables, computer program— is there for the taking through anonymous FTP. The get command is used to retrieve particular files.

Basic FTP Commands

part

1

Command	Settings	Explanation
ftp		start
ftp machine.node.domain	ftp think.com	start and connect
ftp>open machine.node.name	ftp>open think.com	connect (already started)
ftp>is or dir		list contents of directory
ftp>binary	non-text file setting	
ftp>text	text file setting	
ftp>cd	ftp>cd pub	change directory
ftp>get filename	ftp>get libraries.txt	transfer file
ftp>bye		close connection, quit FTP
ftp>close		disconnect, stay in FTP
ftp>quit		quit FTP

Selected File Formats

Files residing on remote computers that are available via FTP are stored in what is commonly referred to as "archives." Files may be stored in text format, but other special formats that require software and/or extra steps for unformatting at your end are also important to know about. The format of a file is usually indicated by a suffix added to a filename. Below are some common formats. If you encounter problems dowloading various formats, or if you need more detail, consult one of the many guides available for your local computer support staff.

Suffix	Format	Software/procedure
.cpt	compacted	UnPack.exe
.gx	GNU compressed	gunzip or gzip
.hqx	binhexed	UnStuffit
.ps	PostScript	use PostScript printer
.sit	stuffed	Stuffit
.tar	Unix tape archive	tar
.txt	ASCII/text readily readable	
.x	Unix compression	Unix "uncompress" command
.zip	zipped	PKUnzip.exe

FTP tip: To be safe, always download your files in binary mode. You can download text files in binary mode, but you cannot download binary files in text mode.

Selected FTP Guides

■ Braun, Eric. (1994). *The Internet Directory*. New York: Fawcett Columbine. ISBN: 0–449–90898–4

■ Carroll, Jim and Broadhead, Rick. (1994). *Canadian Internet Handbook*. Scarborough. ON: Prentice Hall Canada, Inc. ISBN: 0–13–304395–9

■ *The Internet Unleashed*. (1994). Indianapolis, IN: Sams Publishing. ISBN: 0–672–30466-X

■ Hahn, Harley and Stout, Rick. (1994). *The Internet Yellow Pages*. Toronto, ON: Osborne McGraw-Hill ISBN: 0–07–882023–5

■ Rovers, Perry. (1994). *Anonymous FTP Frequently Asked Questions List*. ftp://ftp.eff.org/pub/Net_info/Introductory/Technical/ftp.faq

part

1

Some FTP sites to explore (expressed in URLs):

`ftp://sluaxa.slu.edu/pub/millesjg/newusers.faq`

New Users' FAQ

`ftp://mrcnext.cso.uiuc.edu/pub/etext`

Project Gutenberg: Browse the sub-directories.

`ftp://debra.dgbt.doc.ca/pub/opengov/`
`supreme.court.rulings`

Canadian Supreme Court rulings such as the Rodriguez case

`ftp://debra.dgbt.doc.ca/pub/cbc`

CBC provides access to select news and feature radio programs, list of radio products, and information on how to order transcripts.

`ftp://nigel.msen.com/pub/newsletters/Libraries`

Selection of newsletters about cataloging, indexing, collecting, and preserving books.

`ftp://wuarchive.wustl.edu/systems`

THE place to go for software for your personal computer. Usually quite busy; it may take a few tries to get connected.

part
1

ARCHIE

Archie is a program developed by McGill University that permits the searching of the many FTP archives on the Internet by file name. To do so, telnet to an Archie site. Here are some of the more popular ones.

Telnet to:	archie.ans.net;	login:	archie
Telnet to:	archie.sura.net;	login:	archie
Telnet to:	archie.rutgers.edu	login:	archie
Telnet to:	archie.uqam.ca	login:	archie (français)

Some Basic Archie Commands

Set <variable><value>. Sets variables that affect how your search will be executed. Some good ones to know are:

set search sub	(specifies a substring search without respect to case).
set maxhits n	(sets the maximum number of matches to n).
set malto <address>	(mails the results to <address> rather than printing them on the screen).
prog <string>	searches the Archie database for file names that match <string>.
help	Displays a listing of other commands available in Archie.
bye	Closes the session with the Archie server.

FINDING PEOPLE ON THE NET

The Gopher at yaleinfo.yale.edu provides a menu of tools for finding people on the Internet. Here are some of the more popular tools:

whois	Department of Defense database, also includes Net personalities.
netfind	A very persistent program that uses "finger" to find an email address. You must know the person's name and subdomain to use this program.
phone books	University campus and organization directories.

If you know where the person is (i.e., their domain and subdomain), you can try mailing the postmaster@subdomain.domain and ask for the person's email address. It may take a day or two to get a reply, but this is a sure-fire way to get a response.

SEARCH ENGINES
Generic Internet Address

```
http:/www.oaklandzoo.com to find the Oakland Zoo.
```

These URLs are created by using the name of the company or place with www and a suffix such as com.

part
1

Search Engines

Search engines can be very useful or worthless tools on the Internet depending on knowing how to use them; therefore, you must spend some time learning the proper way to use them. When using Alta Vista the use of quotation marks is essential for finding a site. Example: ("World Trade Center") Forget the quotes and each word will be represented in the list of sites. Your Pyramid Trainer can provide information and tricks for using Internet search engines.

Browsers

`http://www.cc.ukans.edu/lynx_help_main.html`

LYNX is a full featured, World Wide Web (WWW) client for users running curser-addressable, character display devises. It displays hypertext mark up language (HTML), hypertext documents containing links to files residing in the local system. Current versions of Lynx run on UNIX and VMS.

part

1

Veronica

An index and retrieval system which can locate items on most of the Gopher servers on the Internet. The Veronica index contains about 10 million items from approximately 5,500 Gopher servers. Veronica finds resources by searching for words in titles. It does not do a full text search of the contents of the resources; it finds resources whose titles contain specified search word(s). The title is the title of the resource as it appears on the menu of its Gopher server. Veronica is a Gopher client and is chosen from the menu of a Gopher server, and a set of query words or special directives is entered. When the search is finished, the results will be presented as a normal Gopher menu. You may browse the discovered resources in this menu, as you would any other Gopher menu. Try using Veronica to find information on jobs, humor, books, newspapers, anything of interest.

Gopher

A surfboard for the Internet. Gopher provides an easy method to explore the Internet and solves problems of drowning in the vast sea of information. Developed by the University of Minnesota, Gopher provides menu-based access to Internet resources and guides the surfer to a variety of sites. To access a local Gopher menu, simply type *gopher* at the $ or % prompt in your local Internet account.

Gopher tip: Use Veronica to search Gopher space. Veronica is usually grouped on a Gopher with "other Gophers" or "Internet resources."

Lawcrawler

There is a search engine site on the Internet called "Webcrawler." Access that search engine and perform a search using the keyword "Lawcrawler." After you access the Lawcrawler site, there is a fairly diverse menu that allows you to narrow your search even further for such subjects as confidentiality for minors. Search for the keywords "juvenile, proprietary, sealed court documents," and possibly "rights and privileges."

Internet Resources Meta-index

```
http://www.ncsa.uiuc.edu/SDG/Software/Mosaic/
MetaIndex.html
```

This site is a meta-index of various resources, dictionaries, and indices available on the Internet. The site includes a Global Network Academy, a Whole Internet Catalogue, a World Wide Web Virtual Library, and the Clearinghouse for Subject Oriented Internet Resource Guides. New suggestions for new entries on this list may be sent to: mosaic@ncsa. uiuc.edu

part

1

Internet Tools Summary

```
http://www.december.com/net/tools/index.html
```

A collection of information sources about software used on the Internet for network information retrieval, this site is updated continuously. It is popular for use by Internet trainers and students.

Yahoo!

```
http://www.yahoo.com
```

A hierarchical subject-oriented catalog for the World Wide Web and Internet, this popular search engine contains links to humanities, business and economy, recreation and sports, education and reference, and many additional sites.

ArchiPlex

`http://www./erc.nasa.gov/archieplex`

This search engine locates files on anonymous FTP sites on the Internet.

Search Engines: Super PsychNet

`http://users.aol.com/warmgeoff/www.html/#major`

This site contains the following major search engines: Google, Goto.Com, Excite Net Search, Alta Vista Search, AOL Netfind, Aliweb, The Mining Co., Look Smart, Yahoo!, Snap from CNET, Cyber 411, Dogpile, Husky Search, Inference FIND, Profusion, Savvy Search, Starting Point (Metasearch page), All4one, Metafind, SiFMug, Search Spaniel, External Info, Proteus, Global Network Academy Metalibrary, EINet Galaxy, Infoseek, Lycos, Infohiway, Power Search, and HotBot.

Search Engine

`http://www.cmhc.com`

This search engine is devoted to mental health issues.

Mega Go

`http://www.MegaGo.com/`

This search engine is a metasite located in Australia.

Argus Clearinghouse

`http://www.clearinghouse.net`

The Internet library contains a selective collection of topical guides.

Usenet Faq

`http://www.cis.ohio-state.edu:80/text/faq/usenet/`
`FAQ-List.html`

Newsgroup names, archive names, subjects, and keywords are searched on this site.

The Electronic Library

`http://www.elibrary.com`

This search engine contains links to encyclopedias, book stores, international journals, themes/topics, databases, government studies, and magazines. A thirty-day free access period is available.

HealthAtoZ Search Engine

`http://207.87.8.125/categories/COSSML.htm`

This search engine for health and medical resources includes software.

Webivore

`http://www.webivore.com`

Webivore is a search engine dedicated to Internet research.

NovaNet

`http://www.novanet.com`

Novanet is an online suite of courseware, assessments, and communications tools.

WebCrawler

`httpr//www.webcrawler.com`

Dogpile

`http://www.dogpile.com`

SURVIVAL TOOLS AND TIPS

Two useful mailing lists are help-net (listserv@vm.temple.edu) and net-happenings (listserv@is.internic.net). Help-net is a good place to ask questions about the Internet. Net-happenings is a mailing list that discusses new and interesting things happening on the Net.

part

1

The Internet User's Glossary

`ftp://ds.internic.net/rfc/rfc1392.txt`

This resource can help you sort out the techno-babble of the Net people.

December List

`http://www.december.com`

This is a valuable collection of information sources on the Internet mantained by Joh December

Hytelnet

`Access.usask.ca and login as hytelnet.`

This program, developed by Peter Scott of the University of Saskatchewan, presents library resources in an easy-to-use menu interface. When you choose an item from he menu, Hytelnet will give you a short description of the resource and show you how to access it. To use Hytelnet, telnet to:

Subject Indexes

Subject indexes are a group of links which are organized by categories or subjects. They provide easy access to specific Web sites.

Bookmarks

Bookmarks are one of the most useful tools when using the Internet. After a desired Web site is found a bookmark should be immediately created. Bookmarks can be copied to a floppy disk for safe keeping. The floppy disk can be used to import or copy specific bookmarks to any computer.

Survival Tips

1. Buy some good print resources.

2. Set NORMAL on your mailing lists when you will be away for an extended period of time.

3. Keep your directories clean.

4. Keep track of addresses and your favorite sites.

Critical Evaluation

Where Seeing Is Not Always Believing

Typical research resources, such as journal articles, books, and other scholarly works, are reviewed by a panel of experts before being published. At the very least, any reputable publisher takes care to assure that the author is who he or she claims to be and that the work being published represents a reasoned and informed point of view. When anyone can post anything in a Web site or to a newsgroup, the burden of assessing the relevance and accuracy of what you read falls to you. Rumors quickly grow into facts on the Internet simply because stories can spread so rapidly that the "news" seems to be everywhere. Because the Internet leaves few tracks, in no time it's impossible to tell whether you are reading independent stories or the merely same story that's been around the world two or three times. Gathering information on the Internet may be quick, but verifying the quality of information requires a serious commitment.

part

1

Approach researching via the Internet with confidence, however, and not with trepidation. You'll find it an excellent workout for your critical evaluation skills; no matter what career you pursue, employers value an employee who can think critically and independently. Critical thinking is also the basis of problem solving, another ability highly valued by the business community. So, as you research your academic projects, be assured that you're simultaneously developing lifelong expertise.

It's Okay to Be Critical of Others

The first tip for successful researching on the Internet is to always consider your source. A Web site's URL often alerts you to the sponsor of the site. CNN or MSNBC are established news organizations, and you can give the information you find at their sites the same weight you would give to their cablecasts. Likewise, major newspapers operate Web sites with articles reprinted from their daily editions or expanded stories written expressly for the Internet. On the other hand, if you're unfamiliar with the source, treat the information the way you would any new data. Look for specifics—"66 percent of all voters" as opposed to "most voters"—and for information that can be verified—a cited report in another medium or information accessible through a Web site hosted by a credible sponsor—as opposed to generalities or unverifiable claims. Look for independent paths to the same information. This can involve careful use of search engines or visits to newsgroups with both similar and opposing viewpoints. Make sure that the "independent" information you find is truly independent. In newsgroups don't discount the possibility of multiple postings, or that a posting in one group is nothing more than a quotation from a posting in another. Ways to verify independent paths include following sources (if any) back to their origins, contacting the person posting a message and asking for clarification, or checking other media for verification.

In many cases, you can use your intuition and common sense to raise your comfort level about the soundness of the information. With both list servers and newsgroups, it's possible to lurk for a while to develop a feeling for the authors of various postings. Who seems the most authoritarian, and who seems to be "speaking" from emotion or bias? Who seems to know what he or she is talking about on a regular basis? Do these people cite their sources of information (a job or affiliation perhaps)? Do they have a history of thoughtful, insightful postings, or do their postings typically contain generalities, unjustifiable claims, or flames? On Web sites, where the information feels more anonymous, there are also clues you can use to test for authenticity. Verify who's hosting the Web site. If the host or domain name is unfamiliar to you, perhaps a search engine can help you locate more information. Measure the tone and style of the writing at the site. Does it seem consistent with the education level and knowledge base necessary to write intelligently about the subject?

When offering an unorthodox point of view, good authors supply facts, figures, and quotes to buttress their positions, expecting readers to be skeptical of their claims. Knowledgeable authors on the Internet follow these same commonsense guidelines. Be suspicious of authors who expect you to agree with their points of view simply because they've published them on the Internet. In one-on-one encounters, you frequently judge the authority and knowledge of the speaker using criteria you'd be hard pressed to explain. Use your sense of intuition on the Internet, too.

As a researcher (and as a human being), the job of critical thinking requires a combination of healthy skepticism and rabid curiosity. Newsgroups and Web sites tend to focus narrowly on single issues (newsgroups more so than Web sites). Don't expect to find a torrent of opposing views on newsgroup postings; their very nature and reason for existence dampens free-ranging discussions. A newsgroup on *The X-Files* might argue about whether extraterrestrials exist but not whether the program is the premier television show on the air today. Such a discussion

part

1

would run counter to the purposes of the newsgroup and would be a violation of netiquette. Anyone posting such a message would be flamed, embarrassed, ignored, or otherwise driven away. Your research responsibilities include searching for opposing views by visiting a variety of newsgroups and Web sites. A help here is to fall back on the familiar questions of journalism: who, what, when, where, and why.

- **Who** else might speak knowledgeably on this subject? Enter that person's name into a search engine. You might be surprised to find whose work is represented on the Web. (For fun, one of the authors entered the name of a rock-and-roll New York radio disk jockey into MetaCrawler and was amazed to find several pages devoted to the DJ, including sound clips of broadcasts dating back to the sixties, along with a history of his theme song.)

- **What** event might shed more information on your topic? Is there a group or organization that represents your topic? Do they hold an annual conference? Are synopses of presentations posted on the sponsoring organization's Web site?

- **When** do events happen? Annual meetings or seasonal occurrences can help you isolate newsgroup postings of interest.

- **Where** might you find this information? If you're searching for information on wines, for example, check to see if major wine-producing regions, such as the Napa Valley in California or the Rhine Valley in Germany, sponsor Web sites. These may point you to organizations or information that don't show up in other searches. Remember, Web search engines are fallible; they don't find every site you need.

- **Why** is the information you're searching for important? The answer to this question can lead you to related fields. New drugs, for example, are important not only to victims of diseases but to drug companies and the FDA as well.

Approach assertions you read from a skeptic's point of view. See if they stand up to critical evaluation or if you're merely emotionally attached to them. Imagine "What if . . . ?" or "What about . . . ?" scenarios that may disprove or at least call into question what you're reading. Try following each assertion you pull from the Internet with the phrase, "On the other hand. . . ." Because you can't leave the sentence hanging, you'll be forced to finish it, and this will help get you into the habit of critically examining information.

part

1

These are, of course, the same techniques critical thinkers have employed for centuries, only now you are equipped with more powerful search tools than past researchers may have ever imagined. In the time it took your antecedents to formulate their questions, you can search dozens of potential information sources. You belong to the first generation of college students to enjoy both quantity and quality in its research, along with a wider perspective on issues and the ability to form personal opinions after reasoning from a much wider knowledge base. Certainly, the potential exists for the Internet to grind out a generation of intellectual robots, "thinkers" who don't think but who regurgitate information from many sources. Technology always has its good and bad aspects. However, we also have the potential to become some of the most well-informed thinkers in the history of the world, thinkers who are not only articulate but confident that their opinions have been distilled from a range of views, processed by their own personalities, beliefs, and biases. This is one of the aspects of the Internet that makes this era such an exciting combination of humanism and technology.

part

1

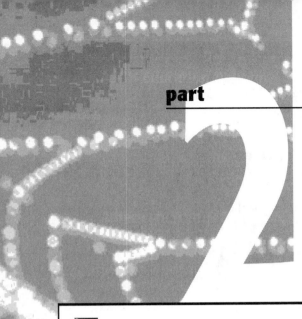

Web Resources
for Counseling

Social Work

MARKETPLACE

The National Association of Social Work

`http://www.naswdc.org`

The major site for NASW information, membership, conferences, this site contains sections on private practice section, careers, licensing, school, issues of diversity, NASW marketplace, email to other professionals, code of ethics, and a listserv site.

Social Work Resources on the Internet

`http://www.uclan.ac.uk/library/lib613a.htm`

This site contains links to health resources on the Internet, midwifery resources, nursing resources on the Internet, gateways to social work, sites of specific interest, and journals and newspapers.

Online Social Work Educational Directory

`http://www.social worker.com/directory.htm`

This site contains the *New Social Worker Magazine,* information about schools which offer social work degree programs, information on the schools themselves, and links to social work schools.

Kearl's Guide to the Sociology of Death Social Work

`http://www.trinity.edu/~mkearl/death-su.html`

The Social Workers Internet Handbook

`http://www.socialworker.com/swintbk.htm`

This site contains ordering information for the *Social Workers Internet Handbook* and information for those who already have the handbook.

Computer Use in Social Services Network

`http://www.uta.edu/cussn/cussn.html`

JOURNALS

Social Work Advocates Forum

`http://www~ssa.uchicago.edu/`

This social work journal is run by students of the University of Chicago's School of Social Work Administration.

PRACTICE AND STAFF DEVELOPMENT

The New Social Worker On Line

`http://www.socialworker.com`

Home of the magazine, *The New Social Worker On Line,* this site contains a guide for selecting and applying to Master of Social Worker programs and a message board for social work careers.

 **Psychiatry**

PROFESSIONAL RESOURCES

Contemporary International Hypnosis

`http://www.wiley.com/psychiatry/burrow.htm`

This site is edited by G. D. Burrows, A. O., and R. Stanley, The University of Melbourne, Australia.

PROFESSIONAL ORGANIZATIONS

American Psychiatric Association

http://www.psych.org

American Psychiatric Nurses Association

http://www.apna.org

This online resource containing legislative action alerts, government links, APNA membership, and professional resources.

National Association of Psychiatric Health Systems

http://www.naphs.org

This behavior health care systems Web site containing membership information and resources.

American Association of Geriatric Psychiatry

http://www.aagpgpa.org

This resource contains an AAGP bookstore, bulletins, consumer information, links to other online information, a member meeting place, and legal notices.

Psycho Oncology

http://www.wiley.com/psychiatry/psycho.htm

The following professional references are available on this site:

- *Counseling People with Cancer,* by Mary Burton, Ph.D.
  http://www.wiley.com/psychiatry/watson.htm
- *A Practical Guide to Psycho-Oncology*—Second Edition,
  by Jennifer Barraclough.
  http://www.wiley.com/psychiatry/barra.htm
- *Cancer and the Family,* edited by L. Baider, C. Cooper, and
  A. Kaplan Denonour.
  http://www.wiley/psychiatry/baider.htm
- *Psycho Oncology Journal*
  http://www.interscience.wiley.com/jpages/1057-9249

part
2

Psychiatric Disabilities, Employment, and the Americans with Disabilities Act Background Paper

http://www.clark.net/pub/klaatu/ada_ota.html

This site offers a paper to evaluate current efforts under the ADA in the area of psychiatric disabilities and employment. This study was conducted by the Office of Technology Assessment.

AACP Community Psychiatrist

http://www.pitt.edu/~kthomp

A publication of the American Association of Community Psychiatrists, this site contains links with additional psychiatric resources for community mental health.

American Association of Medical Review Office

http://www.aamro.com

This site contains links with educational programs, certification information, resources, and seminars.

DSM-IV Diagnoses and Codes

http://uhs.bsd.uchicago.edu/~bhsiung/tips/
dsm4a.html

This is an alphabetical listing of diagnoses and codes. There is also a corresponding numerical listing.

SuperPsychNet

http://users.aol.com/warmgeoff/homepage.html/
#SPNNavigator

This site serves as a resource center for major psychology, mental health, addiction, and resource sites. Also included are: statistical software, analysis tools, a social sciences database, links to questionnaires, experiments on the Net, online literature, search tools, and a collection of search engines.

Professional Connections

LISTSERVS

CataList

`http://segate.sunet.se/lists/listref-eng.html`

A catalogue of 26,789 public listserv lists on the Internet. Search for mailing lists of interest, and get information about listserv host sites.

Listserve list by Subject

`http://www.mste.uiuc.edu/listserves/subjectsearch.html`

Global School Psychology Network

`http://www.dac.neu.edu/cp/consult/`

An innovative Internet Community dedicated to peer support, problem-solving assistance, professional development, and research.

Treatment

`http://journals.apa.org/treatment`
`http://www.psycoh.com/websight.shtml`

Edited by Martin E. P. Seligman and Donald F. Klein, *Treatment* is also free and comes with an email discussion list for subscribers to discuss the latest in psychological and psychiatric outcome/treatment research. Also included is some information on the Planetree model of patient-centered health care that is emerging as an alternative to traditional managed care.

Counseling Today

`http://www.counseling.org/ctonline`

The Web version of *Counseling Today* has been revamped with a new look and more importantly is updated throughout the week with the latest news affecting professional counseling.

part

2

Human Rights Education Listserv

```
http://www.un.org/Pubs/CyberSchoolBus/humanrights
```

The UN CyberSchoolBus has initiated a discussion mail list (listserv) as part of its "Human Rights in Action" project. When you register for this project, you are automatically added to the list and will be receiving a confirmation message shortly from the list provider. The purpose of this discussion group is to examine human rights within the context of education. Specifically, the discussion will attempt to examine the teaching of and learning about human rights within schools and the classroom.

CESNET-L

A moderated listserv concerning counselor education and supervision, discussions about research, theory, and development of program applications pertinent to counselor education or supervision are encouraged. The listserv is concerned with the preparation and supervision of counselors in agencies, school settings, and private practice. To subscribe: subscribe CESNET-L your email address

COUNSGRADS

COUNSGRADS has been developed to help graduate students from across the country communicate with one another. Students can talk about classes, internships, papers, and ideas about the profession. To sign up, send an email to: counsgrads@lists.acs.ohio-state.edu with the following in the body of the message: subscribe COUNSGRADS jane smith

Listserv Directories

```
http://www.liszt.com
http://www.mailbase.ac.uk
http://www.siec.k12.in.us/~west/edu/list.htm
http://psychcentral.com/mail.htm
http://www.reference.com
```

Government Listing

```
http://www.ed.gov
```

This U.S. Department of Education site includes an education kiosk, community updates, an EdInfo/listserv, Ed initiatives, Ed press releases, Ed publications published within the last ninety days, satellite town meetings, speeches, and testimonies, White House education press releases and statements, National Center for Education statistics, and school-to-work, safe and drug-free schools, Office of Vocational and Adult Education, and National Library of Education information.

At Health, Inc.

`http://www.athealth.com`

This newsletter is distributed to over 7,300 mental health professionals

DISCUSSION GROUPS AND BULLETIN BOARDS

The Network Observer

The file contains a single article from *The Network Observer,* entitled "The Art of Getting Help," which offers some guidelines about using Internet discussion groups to ask for assistance with research projects and the like. For a much longer paper that describes how to use the Net to build a professional community, send a message that looks like this:

To: rre-request@weber.ucsd.edu
Subject: archive send network

part

2

Network Observer is distributed through the Red Rock Eater News Service. To subscribe to RRE, send a message to the RRE server, rre-request@weber.ucsd.edu, whose subject line reads "subscribe first name last name;" for example "Subject: subscribe Jane Doe." For more information about the Red Rock Eater, send a message to that same address with a subject line of "help." For back issues, use a subject line of "archive send index."

School Counselors' Discussion Group

`Techsc@cblist.org`

Internet discussion group/mailing list for school counselors and counselor educators that focuses exclusively on the opportunities and implications of using emerging technology in school counseling.

Technology and School Counseling

`techsc@cblist.org`

The purpose of this discussion group is to discuss methods, ideas, and resources for using technology in guidance and counseling-related activities. Group members will be encouraged to share helpful Web sites, create Internet projects with other schools, suggest Internet-based activities, express opinions and concerns about the use of technology, ask questions about purchasing software or hardware, get help with the design of their personal and/or guidance department's Web page, announce technology grants, and anything else related to the subject. This group is open to any school counselor (K-12) and counselor educator. To sign-up, go to: http://www.cblist.org. After entering the discussion group area, click on GUIDANCE, then click on "Techsc" (technology in school counseling) and follow the directions. To send a message to group members, simple email the message to: techsc@cblist.org

COUNSELING DISCUSSION GROUPS

http://www.csun.edu/~hfedp001/counseling_listservs.html

This site contains links to various discussion groups. Clicking on a link will allow you to email the group directly. Specific instructions for subscribing to some of the better groups follow.

CESNET-L (Counselor Education and Supervision Network).

Counselor educators, supervisors, and students discuss research, theory, and practice related to a wide variety of professional counseling and supervision issues. To sign on, send the message: subscribe CESNET-L.

ACCA-L (American College Counseling Association)

The emphasis of this list is on counseling issues with college students and the developmental and psychological issues they face while in college. College counselors and others who deal with this age group are the primary subscribers. To sign on, send the message: subscribe ACCA-L.

ICN (International Counselor Network)

This network is for counselors working in all specialty areas. Topics range widely, including such issues as self-esteem, multicultural issues, program development, career planning, play theory, professional issues, and more. To sign on, send the message: subscribe ICN.

C-PSYCH (Cross Cultural Psychology)

This is a forum for all individuals interested in cross-cultural psychology and its intertwining disciplines. To subscribe, send a message: subscribe C-PSYCH (your first name, your last name).

PSYCGRAD (Psychology Graduate Student Project)

This list informally discusses issues of relevance to graduate students within the field of psychology and also publishes a more formal journal including student papers. To sign on, send the message: subscribe PSYCGRAD.

EAP (Employee Assistance Counselors Net Discussion List)

EAP is a list which discusses any aspect of employee assistance counseling and psychological interventions in the workplace. To sign on, send the message: subscribe EAP.

CARDEVNET (Career Development Network Discussion List)

CARDEVNET is a list for the discussion of issues relating to career development. To sign on, send the message: subscribe CARDEVNET.

PSYCH-COUN

This is a discussion group for people who are interested in theoretical or research issues in counseling and psychotherapy. Students and researchers are both welcome. To sign on, send the message: subscribe PSYCH-COUNS.

Transcultural-Psychology

This list discusses the different views of mental disorders that exist among cultures. To sign on, send the message: subscribe TRANSCULTURAL-PSYCHOLOGY.

Survival

This list discusses topics related to domestic violence, child abuse, sexual assault and crisis/trauma intervention. The goal of the list is to provide a safe information and support network for victims of abuse and individuals who work in the field of abuse. To subscribe, send the message: subscribe SURVIVAL.

GROUPSTUFF at Indiana University

This is a list for group workers. To subscribe, leave subject line blank, type subscribe GROUPSTUFF Internet address in the message section, then

part

2

send. Note: you must use your Internet address rather than your given name in subscribing to this list. If you have difficulty, contact Rex Stockton.

Group-Psychology

This is a list for group-therapists about processes and stages, models for group therapy, leadership and coleadership, special populations, and techniques. To subscribe, leave subject line blank, type subscribe GROUP-PSYCHOTHERAPY first name last name in the message section, then send. If you have difficulty, contact Haim Weinberg.

NETPSY: Internet Psychology

This is a list for discussion of psychological services on the Internet. To subscribe, leave the subject line blank, type subscribe NETPSY first name last name in the message section, then send.

PSCHYNEWS

This mental health newsletter for mental health students and professionals is accessed at: listserv@vm1.nodak.edu. To subscribe, leave the subject line blank, type subscribe PNI first name last name in the message section, then send.

Family Therapy Networker

Family Therapy Networker Magazine has a free online mailing list where you can discuss matters related to family therapy with practitioners and Networker staff. In the subject line enter: subscribe. In the body enter: subscribe ftnetwork@intr.net.

Psychotherapy Usenet Group

```
news:sci.psychology.psychotherapy
```

School Counseling Bulletin Board

```
http://www.schoolcounselor.com
```

Go to the bottom of the page and click on the BBS button. Future announcements about the schoolcounselor.com Web site will offer a newsletter, counseling link database, and more.

TREATMENT SOFTWARE

The Earley Corporation

http://www.earleycorp.com/

The Earley Corporation is a developer of software which assists mental health providers.

Therascribe by Wiley & Sons

http://www.therapyshop.com/TheraScribe/

Therascribe can produce treatment plans which are outstanding and contain all elements of JCAHO. Windows-based design.

Therapist Helper by Brand Software, Inc.

http://www.quicdoc.com/Therapist_Helper/
therapist_helper.htm

This site contains billing and practice management software for mental health professionals. A full working demo may be downloaded.

part

2

PsyJourn Home Page

http://www.psyjourn.com

This site features software products designed to be used by mental Health treatment professionals.

Therapist Traveler for the Palm Pilot

www.helper.com/products/traveler

This program enables providers to add new appointments to Traveler, make schedule changes, use and update contact information, and then synchronize this information with Therapist Helper at the touch of a button. With Therapist Traveler, you can have the most current and most important practice management information with you wherever you go.

Clinical Supervision Models

http://www.nbcc.org/

This is the NBCC Web site for their supervision certification and model.

The Values Realization Institute

http://www.vrf.org/

This nonprofit organization posts the following mission statement: The Values Realization Institute creates, supports, and empowers a network of people committed to using the Values Realization principles and concepts to positively impact the quality of life in our world community.

PROFESSIONAL ORGANIZATIONS

The American Psychological Association

http://www.apa.org

The American Psychological Society

http://www.psychologicalscience.org

Association for Specialists in Group Work

http://coe.colstate.edu/asgw/

American Association for Marriage and Family Therapists

http://www.aamft.org/

American Counseling Association

http://www.counseling.org

California Association of Marriage and Family Therapists

http://www.camft.org/

American Association for Therapeutic Humor

http://www.aath.org/

Association for Multicultural Counseling and Development

http://www.sagepub.com/series_multicultural.htm

Academy of Counseling Psychology

http://www.hometown.net/academy/academy.htm

Association for Death Education and Counseling

`http://www.adec.org/`

Association for Humanistic Psychology

`http://www.ahpweb.org/`

Association for Transpersonal Psychology

`http://www.atpweb.org/`

Canadian Association for Music Therapy

`http://www.musictherapy.ca/`

American Association of Pastoral Counselors

`http://www.aapc.org/`

National Coalition of Arts Therapy Associations

`http://www.ncata.com/`

Sufi Psychological Association

`http://www.sufi-psychology.org`

part

2

Researching Online

BOOKSTORES

Amazon.com

`http://www.amazon.com`

This excellent online book store offers some great savings!

Jason Aronson, Inc

`http://www.aronson.com`

This site offers discounts on over 1,000 titles of works in psychotherapy, alcoholism, drug abuse, cognitive therapy, and child therapy, plus the choice of one free book for each one offered.

Dual Diagnosis Online Dictionary of Mental Health

http://www.human-nature.com/odmh/dual.html

Sciacca hosts this Web site for co-occurring mental illness and substance disorders. Complete articles and chapters may be read and downloaded. It also contains a search engine and mailing lists.

ELECTRONIC JOURNALS

Electronic Journals and Periodicals in Psychology and Related Fields

http://www.yu.edu/ferkauf/lists/journal.htm

Here you will find an alphabetical listing of electronic journals found on the Web.

Brown University Library of Electronic Resources

http://www.brown.edu/Facilities/University_Library/
electronic/Subject/

ERIC Articles

The latest quarterly update to the *ERIC* (Educational Resources Information Center) *Digest* database features sixty-seven full-text short reports aimed at education professionals and the broader education community. Each report includes an overview of an education topic of current interest and offers references for further information. Sample titles include *Improving Ethnic and Racial Relations in the Schools, Libraries and Democracy, Social Identity and the Adult ESL Classroom,* and *A Paradigm Shift from Instruction to Learning.* Users can search the entire ERIC Digests database from the index page. ERIC, part of the National Library of Education (NLE), is a nationwide education information system sponsored by the U.S. Department of Education's Office of Educational Research and Improvement (OERI). The URL for new additions to *ERIC Digest's* database is: http://www.ed.gov/databases/ERIC_Digests/index/edo98b.html. *ERIC Digest's* Index Page is found at: http://www.ed.gov/databases/ERIC_Digests/index.

Sample ERIC Articles.   This digest was created by ERIC, The Educational Resources Information Center. For more information about ERIC, contact ACCESS ERIC: 1–800-LET-ERIC.

ERIC Digest. "Helping Young Children Deal with Anger." Author: Marion, Marian. ERIC Clearinghouse on Elementary and Early Childhood Education. Champaign, IL. ED414077 97

Helping Children Develop Self-Regulatory Skills. Realizing that the children in their care have a very limited ability to regulate their own emotions, teachers of infants and toddlers do a lot of self-regulation "work." As children get older, adults can gradually transfer control of the self to children so that they develop self-regulatory skills.

Encouraging Children to Label Feelings of Anger. Teachers and parents can help young children produce a label for their anger by teaching them that they are having a feeling and that they can use a word to describe their angry feeling. A permanent record (a book or chart) can be made of lists of labels for anger (e.g., mad, irritated, annoyed), and the class can refer to it when discussing angry feelings.

Encouraging Children to Talk About Anger-Arousing Interactions. Preschool children better understand anger and other emotions when adults explain emotions (Denham, Zoller, and Couchoud, 1994). When children are embroiled in an anger-arousing interaction, teachers can help by listening without judging, evaluating, or ordering them to feel differently.

part

2

Using Books and Stories About Anger to Help Children Understand and Manage Anger. Well-presented stories about anger and other emotions validate children's feelings and give information about anger (Jalongo, 1986; Marion, 1995). It is important to preview all books about anger because some stories teach irresponsible anger management.

SARA

This service is provided by Carfax Publishing. Contents pages for all of the journals, for those in a subject cluster, or for just one title can be requested, all free of charge! To register for this complimentary service either:

1. Access the Carfax Home Page (http://www.carfax.co.uk), enter SARA, and follow the on-screen instructions, or

2. Send an email to SARA@carfax.co.uk with the word "info" in the body of the message.

FIRNmail

FIRN's electronic mail (email) service features an easy to use word processing editor, online messaging, interfaces to other email systems world wide, access to limited number of Internet services, and a conferencing system which serves as a bulletin board service. The phone number for FIRN Support Staff/Help desk is (800–749–3476)

PROFESSIONAL RESOURCES

Guides to Internet Resources

http://www.clearinghouse.net

The Argus Clearinghouse offers a large collection of guides to Internet resources categorized by topic.

Multicultural Aspects of Counseling

http://www.sagepub.com/series_multicultural.htm

This site offers links to volumes in a series by Paul Pederson, Ph.D., Syracuse University. Volumes are related to multicultural issues and are written by a variety of counselors and Educators.

Federal Government Information

http://www.lib.lsu.edu/gov/fedgov.html

This is the Louisiana State University Libraries United States Federal Government Agencies Page.

Library Catalogs

http://www.library.usask.ca/hywebcat

WebCATS, from the University of Saskatchewan Libraries, is a directory of library catalogs which can be searched via the Web. WebCATS is organized for searching geographically, by type of library, and by library catalog vendor.

Library of Congress

http://www.lcweb.loc.gov/catalog

This site provides access to the holdings of the Library of Congress, United States Government copyright files, federal legislation, foreign law, and gateway access to many other library catalogs.

Update Your Search Skills

```
http://www.zdnet.com/products/filter/guide/
0,7267,6000176,00.html
```

The ZDNet Web site has put together a series of articles intended to help users search the Net more efficiently.

Brief Counseling That Works: A Solution-Focused Approach for School Counselors

```
Email: order@corwin.sagepub.com
```

Department Home Page Human Development Resource Center

```
http://www.hec.ohio-state.edu/famlife/index.htm
```

National Network for Family Resiliency

```
http://www.nnfr.org
```

Counseling Center Village

```
http://ub-counseling.buffalo.edu/ccv.html
```

part **2**

1 AND 2 CURRICULUM

MARCO

A counselor-owned and operated company, MARCO is accessible at 1–800–448–2197. Their offerings include:

- Lions Quest Skills
- Here's Looking at You 2000
- The Name Game
- Facts About Friends
- Handling Anger
- Study Skills 1 & 2
- Classroom Guidance Activities

- Classroom Guidance Primary and Intermediate
- 102 Tools for Teachers & Counselors, Too.

Paperbacks for Education

Bibliotherapy books arranged by topic that helps with selecting books to use in class and groups. 1-800-227-2591.

Connecting with Others: Lessons for Teaching Social and Emotional Competence

http://www.schoolcounselor.org.

One volume is for K–2 and the other is 3–5. Access the ASCA Essentials Publications catalogue online for other titles. An elementary counselor, Judy Swaim, lists the books and resources she uses in her counseling program in Alabama. You can get to Judy's Web site off the K–12 counseling department LINKS on the ACSA site.

The School Counselor's Book of Lists

This book is available for examination free for thrity days by calling 1-800-288-4745. The order # is C1293–4. If you decide to purchase the book, it is $32.95 plus postage.

Community Peacemakers 1999 Edition

http://emf.net/~swaaden/peacemaker.

This update, geared toward educators, is full of counseling material for classroom use, bulletin boards, and handouts. The site provides information about archived materials as well as the '99 update. For more information about the program's organizer, Community Peacemakers, please send an email to: compeace@concentric.net For immediate access to on-line past editions and articles since April 1998, use their Web site and "click" current month express and then "click" past editions. Items from the heart in this edition include:

1. *This is How I Want to Live My Life in 1999,* by Unknown, Off the Internet, 1998.

2. *Creating Peace Within: Conflict Release the Way Kids Do It,* by Eddy Buchanan, Heart Dance, Page 18, July 1995.

3. *Decide to Network,* by Dr. Robert Muller, Former Undersecretary General of the United Nations.

PROFESSIONAL SERVICES

American Academy of Pediatrics

http://www.aap.org

This Web site is committed to the attainment of optimal physical, mental, and social health for all infants, children, adolescents, and young adults.

The American Psychiatric Association

http://www.psych.org

The American Psychiatric Association is a national medical specialty society whose 40,500 physician members specialize in the diagnosis and treatment of mental and emotional illnesses and substance use disorders.

American Psychological Association (APA)

http://www.apa.org:80/divisons/div28/index.html

This is the home page for the Division of Psychopharmacology and Substance Abuse of the American Psychological Association. Of interest to psychologists practicing in the drug abuse field may be the Web site for the APA College of Professional Psychology.

American Psychological Society (APS)

http://www.psychologicalscience.org

Advancing the scientific discipline and the giving away of psychology in the public interest is the aim of this site.

American Public Health Association

http://www.apha.org

The American Public Health Association (APHA) is the oldest and largest organization of public health professionals in the world, representing more than 50,000 members from over fifty occupations of public health. The Association and its members have been influencing policies and setting priorities in public health since 1872.

part

2

Brian Disorders Network

http://www.brainnet.org

The Brain Disorders Network is sponsored by the National Foundation for Brain Research.

The Centers for Disease Control and Prevention (CDC)

http://www.cdc.gov

The Centers for Disease Control and Prevention (CDC), located in Atlanta, Georgia, USA, is an agency of the Public Health Service, in the Department of Health and Human Services. Its mission is to promote health and quality of life by preventing and controlling disease, injury, and disability.

Coalition of Hispanic Health and Human Services Organizations

part 2

http://www.cossmho.org

Its mission is to improve the health and well-being of all Hispanic communities throughout the United States. COSSMHO is the sole organization focusing on the health, mental health, and human services needs of the diverse Hispanic communities.

The Institute of Behavioral Research at TCU

http://www.ibr.tcu.edu

The Institute of Behavioral Research (IBR) at TCU conducts evaluations of drug abuse and addiction services. Special attention is given to assessing and analyzing individual functioning, treatment delivery, and engagement process, and their relationships to outcomes. Treatment improvement protocols developed and tested emphasize cognitive and behavioral strategies for programs in community-bases as well as criminal justice settings. Its people, projects, publications, and training programs are described, and a variety of data collection forms are available for downloading.

National Criminal Justice Reference Service (NCJRS)

http://www.whitehousedrugpolicy.gov
http://www.ncjrs.org/ndjhome.htm

The National Criminal Justice Reference Service (NCJRS) is one of the most extensive sources of information on criminal and juvenile justice in the world, providing services to an international community of policymakers and professionals. NCJRS is a collection of clearing-houses supporting all bureaus of the U.S. Department of Justice, Office of Justice Programs: the National Institute of Justice, the Office of Juvenile Justice and Delinquency Prevention, the Bureau of Justice Statistics, the Bureau of Justice Assistance, the Office for Victims of Crime, and the OJP Program Offices. It also supports the Office of National Drug Control Policy. National Families in Action (NFIA).

National Families in Action (NFIA)

http://www.emory.edu/NFIA

A private, nonprofit membership organization founded in 1977. It helped create and lead the parent movement, the first tier of the prevention movement that drove drug use down by two-thirds among adolescents and young adults between 1979 and 1992. Its goal is to help parents prevent drug abuse in their families and communities.

National Library of Medicine

http://www.nlm.nih.gov

The National Library of Medicine is the world's largest library dealing with a single scientific/professional topic. It cares for over 4.5 million holdings (including books, journal, reports, manuscripts, and audio-visual items).

National Board for Certified Counselors (NBCC)

http://www.nbcc.org/wire.htm

This site contains listings for information on state and national credentialing, graduate student updates, bulletins, and a newsletter with NCC LINC. Also included is an RACC bulletin which contains information on summer fellowships.

The Internet: A Tool for Career Planning

http://www.ncda.org

Published by NCDA (National Career Development Association), *The Internet: A Tool for Career Planning,* is coauthored by Joann Harris-

part

2

Bowlsbey, Margaret Riley Kikel, and James P. Sampson, Jr. Single copies are 17.95, 14.95 for NCDA members. Order number is #72656.

Career Counseling Resources

CAREER GUIDANCE

ACAeNews

`http://www.counseling.org/enews/volume_2/0202a.htm`

ACAeNews begins a two-part series on anticipated changes in career guidance and counseling in schools. Changing United States demographics demand broader perspectives of professionals who must prepare the next generation of workers. Part one addresses key historical issues, explores the role of the school counselor in career counseling, and compares career education versus career guidance.

NBCC News Wire

`http://www.nbcc.org/wire.htm`

This site lists the *USA Today* Career Center under *USA Today* Online. Career information is offered to National Certified Career Counselors. Each week an NBCC answers career questions from people around the United States and from *USA Today* Career Center's "Ask a Counselor" column. Readers are invited to ask questions to be answered by an NBCC.

College is Possible

`http://www.CollegeIsPossible.org`

Created by the Coalition of America's Colleges, this site is offered as a guide for parents and students to information and advice on higher education, especially with regard to financial matters. The site is composed of three primary sections: Preparing for College, Choosing the Right College, and Paying for College. The first section offers a ten-step guide (beginning with pre-school), recommended secondary school courses, and an electronic and print resource library.

Career/College Counseling Links

`http://www2.widener.edu/~keh0002/workshop.html`

Dozens of career and college counseling links are available at this site:

Internet Guide for College Bound Students

`http://www.amazon.com`

Published by The College Board, the book is available online (www.amazon.com) or in bookstores. Chapters contain resources for college exploration.

The Student Center

`http://www.counseling.org/enews/volume_2/0202b.htm`

Volunteering with professionals and agencies. Developing real working relationships with educators, professionals, and agencies as a volunteer can be a helpful way to gain valuable experiences and maybe get an edge in your future job hunt.

part

2

Lynn Friedman, Ph.D.'s Web Site

`http://www.andrew.cmu.edu/~lf0j/index.html`

This site provides answers to questions about the trials and tribulations in the workplace, dealing with challenging interpersonal situations, negotiating salary, finding a better job, and establishing and pursuing life goals at work and in life.

Weddles Web Guide

`http://www.careers.wsj.com`

A most excellent resource, Weddles Web Guide is a listing of online job databases.

Career Aptitude Test/ Career Development Software (Elementary–College)

`Email: Dmking1@aol.com`

Careerware. Computerized aptitude test for 8th grade to adult known as the Career Aptitude Survey. The CAS, which is a timed/standardized/

computerized aptitude test, encompasses 5 areas: Verbal Comprehension, Numerical Ability, Visual Speed and Accuracy, Space Visualization, and Numerical Reasoning. Also available: a broad spectrum of computerized career development software available for upper elementary, middle school, high school, college, and beyond, as well as many other supplemental products necessary for building a successful career center or career program at your site.

EXPLORE

Email: brasel@act.org

ACT's eighth grade program includes a workbook in which students develop a four year plan based on the results of the Interest Inventory, UNIACT, and the results of their achievement scores in English, math, reading, and science reasoning.

Career Counseling Netserve

part

2

Email: cardevnet-request@world.std.com

This site lists counseling discussion groups. From there you can click on CARDEVNET (Career Development Network Discussion List). To sign on, send the message (in the body, no subject), subscribe (no quotation marks).

VOCATIONAL EDUCATION/SCHOOL-TO-WORK

National Center for Research in Vocational Education

http://vocserve.berkeley.edu/SkillsPage.html

This site includes full texts of newsletters, monographs, and other reports produced by NCRVE. It also includes skill standards links, a calendar of events, and a listing of school-to-work technical assistance providers. A mini-catalogue can be found at:

New York Department of Labor

http://www.labor.state.ny.us/html/

This site focuses on youth career and has information about choosing a career, acquiring needed skills, finding a job, and tools for educators. It also has links to working papers and a career resource library.

National School-To-Work Learning and Information Center

http://www.stw.ed.gov

This site includes a variety of information about initiatives, resources, grants, technical assistance providers, research, and events.

Florida School-To-Work Information Navigator

http://www.flstw.fsu.edu

This Florida STW clearinghouse site includes information on business partners, conferences and workshops, a directory, grants legislation, a newsletter, and resources. For a conference calendar, brochures in Spanish, exemplary program highlights, Web-based videos, and information about free telecasts, go to this site, which also links to esources for grants and funding information, legislative updates, and evaluation materials.

Education Week

http://www.edweek.org/context/topics/work.htm

The *Education Week* newspaper has a site containing school-to-work articles from its archives. It also provides other print and Web resources on school-to-work.

part

2

Minnesota School-to-Work: School Activities

http://children.state.mn.us/stw/school.html/best/
Teacher.htm

Find out why Minnesota's School-to-Work program is so effective. Not only do students visit workplaces and perform real work there, but so do teachers, as Brian A. Bottge and Lynne S. Osterman discuss in *Bringing the Workplace to the Classroom.*

PORTFOLIOS

Chuck Eby's Counseling Resources

http://www.cybercomm.net/~chuck/guide.html

This counseling resources Web site is for students, parents, and counselors. It contains college information, financial aid information, sources for study skill help, career information, and resources for counselors.

Federal Employment Opportunities

http://www.usajobs.opm.gov

This site contains job listing from the Veterans Administration.

HealthCareerWeb

http://www.healthcareerweb.com

This site provides services for job seekers and includes a job search feature, a resume database, and a free job-match service. The site also markets products.

America's Career InfoNet

http://www.acinet.org

This site offers registered users America's Job Bank listing of thousands of job vacancies and America's Talent Bank for employers in search of a database of resumes.

CAREER DEVELOPMENT COMPUTER SOFTWARE

Choices

http://www.can.ibm.com/ism/careerware

This very affordable and a highly effective career development product for high school students does assessments, occupational searches, and college searches (with Internet connections to college Web pages and on-line applications). Included are: a letter writer component for colleges and scholarships, a scholarship database (with Internet connections to various scholarships and financial aid Web sites), a graduate school database (with same Internet capabilities as undergrad schools), connection to America's Job Bank, connection to America's Talent Bank, a resume builder, an interviewing component, ability to build a very professional career portfolio for the students. . . . The list goes on and on. And the best thing is Choices is user friendly and can be put on as many computers at your site as you like all for under $950.00 (annual site license).

COIN

http://www.coinep.com/

This Guidance Program comes in both Windows and Mac platforms. It is a very complete program. COIN Educational Products, Inc, can be reached at 1-800-274-8515.

School Counseling Resources

GUIDANCE CURRICULUM

Classroom Guidance Activities

http://www.educationalmedia.com/home.html-ssi

Elementary School Counselors will enjoy this Sourcebook. (There is also an edition available for Secondary School Counselors.) The authors are; Joe Wittmer, Ph.D., Diane W. Thompson, Ed.S., and Larry C. Loesch, Ph.D. If you would like to order a copy of this book you can write or call the publisher at Educational Media Corporation, PO Box 21311, Minneapolis, MN 55421–0311, (612) 781-0088. The cost of the book is $24.95.

part

2

I Am Responsible

http://www.scholastic.com/index.htm

This integrated theme unit connects classroom learning and life lessons.

We Are Family

http://www.scholastic.com/lessonrepro/lessonplans/theme/fam23.htm

This integrated theme unit explores all kinds of families. You can choose from Kindergarten through grade 1, grades 2 to 3, and grades 4 to 8.

Test Anxiety and Stress Workshops

http://ub-counseling.buffalo.edu/ccv.html

The Counseling Center Village. A good resource for workshops, with outlines on stress management and test anxiety.

Relaxation Training

Available on http://www.amazon.com:

- *Don't Despair on Thursdays!* The Children's Grief-Management Book (The Emotional Impact Series). Adolph Moser, et. al., School & Library Binding, 1998. Usually ships in twenty-four hours.
- *Don't Feed the Monster on Tuesdays!* The Children's Self-Esteem Book. Adolph J. Moser, et. al., School & Library Binding, 1991. Usually ships in twenty-four hours.
- *Don't Pop Your Cork on Mondays!* The Children's Anti-Stress Book. Adolph J. Moser, Dav Pilkey (Illustrator), School & Library Binding, 1988. Usually ships in twenty-four hours.
- *Don't Rant and Rave on Wednesdays!* The Children's Anger-Control Book. Adolph Moser, et. al., School & Library Binding, 1994.

Bibliotherapy in Elementary Schools

`http://www.indiana.edu/~eric_rec/ieo/bibs/`
`bibl-ele.html`

This is a useful site for conducting bibliocounseling with elementary students.

NBCC News Wire

`www.nbcc.org/wire.htm`

The Web site of the National Board for Certified Counselors, Incorporated, has current updates, news, and bulletins. Approved continuing education providers as well as a NBCC approved home study program are listed.

Susquehanna Institute

`http://www.susquehanna-institute.com`

Help support free and low-cost counseling by ordering books, CDs, videos, and games.

New One-Stop for Department Publications

`http://www.ed.gov/pubs/edpubs.html`

Ed Pubs is the Department of Education's one-stop shop for information products. Ed Pubs (short for Education Publications Center) is the place to call for publications, brochures, videos, CD-ROMs, posters, bookmarks, and other Ed products. Ed Pubs include online ordering via the Internet, a searchable database that includes all Ed products, a customer call center, and an automated inventory system for Ed personnel. Ed Pubs customer service representatives (including Spanish speaking representatives) are available from 9 A.M. to 6 P.M. (ET), Monday through Friday. You may call any time to leave a voicemail request or to use the fax-on-demand service.

Education World

http://db.education-world.com/perl/browse?cat_id=589

ERIC/CASS (Under ERIC)

http://www.uncg.edu/~ericcas2

Clearinghouse (ERIC/CASS). The original clearinghouse was established in 1966 by Dr. Garry R. Walz at the University of Michigan and has been in continuous operation since that date. Its scope area includes school counseling, school social work, school psychology, mental health counseling, marriage and family counseling, career counseling, and student development, as well as parent, student, and teacher education in the human resources area. Topics covered by ERIC/CASS include training, supervision, and continuing professional development; human services and mental health professionals; counseling theories, methods, and practices; the roles of counselors, social workers, and psychologists in all the education settings at all levels; career planning and development; self-esteem and self-efficacy; marriage and family counseling; and counseling services to special populations such as substance abusers, pregnant teenagers, students at risk, and public offenders.

part

2

Fifty Research Syntheses have been added recently to a full-text searchable database of 2,000 such syntheses on the Department's Web site at: http://www.ed.gov/databases/ERIC_Digests/index.

The following are the titles of the 50 ERIC Digests:

File Name	File Title
ed419326	Rights & Responsibilities of Parents of Children with Disabilities.
ed419385	Secondary Newcomer Programs: Helping Recent Immigrants Prepare for School Success.
ed419624	Loneliness in Young Children.
ed419625	Failure Syndrome Students.

ed419632	Father Involvement in Schools.
ed420302	The Benefits of Information Technology.
ed420303	Internet Resources for K-8 Students.
ed420305	An Introduction to Internet Resources for K–12 Educators. Part I: Information Resources, Update 1998.
ed420306	An Introduction to Internet Resources for K–12 Educators. Part II: Question Answering, Listservs, Discussion Groups, Update 1998.
ed420897	Creating a Learning Organization.
ed421179	Forces Motivating Institutional Reform.
ed421180	Using Technology in Remedial Education.
ed421181	Responding to Accountability Mandates.
ed421281	Motivation and Middle School Students.
ed421447	A Global Perspective on Human Rights Education.
ed421480	Promoting Stress Management: The Role of Comprehensive School Health Programs.
ed421481	Service-Learning and Teacher Education.
ed421483	True and Quasi-Experimental Designs.
ed421484	Statewide Assessment Programs: Policies and Practices for the Inclusion of Limited English Proficient Students.
ed421485	Designing Structured Interviews for Educational Research.
ed421486	Herzberg's Theory of Motivation and Maslow's Hierarchy of Needs.
ed416940	Effective Policies for Remedial Education.
ed416941	Faculty and Staff Development.
ed417123	Trends in Peace Education.
ed417124	Global Education: Internet Resources.
ed417244	Improving School Violence Prevention Programs through Meaningful Evaluation.
ed417501	Reducing the Disproportionate Representation of Minority Students in Special Education.
ed417515	School-Wide Behavioral Management Systems.
ed418249	New Perspectives on Mentoring.
ed418654	Faculty Workload Studies: Perspectives, Needs, and Future Directions.
ed418832	Building School-to-Work Systems in Rural America.
ed419029	Recent Changes in School Desegregation.
ed419030	The Challenges of Parent Involvement Research.
ed419031	Parent Engagement as a School Reform Strategy.

part
2

Access Eric

http://www.accesseric.org/

This is the gateway to the Internet sites of the Educational Resources Information Center (ERIC).

AskEric/Lesson Plans

http://ericir.syr.edu/Virtual/Lessons

The AskERIC Virtual Library contains hundreds of lesson plans, including, but not limited to, language arts, mathematics, social studies, and science. Also included are lesson plans from School Library Media Activities Monthly, Newton's Apple Educators Guides, and Crossroads: K16 American History Curriculum.

AskERIC Toolbox

http://ericir.syr.edu/Qa/Toolbox

This site showcases favorite resources of AskERIC's question-answering service.

Benard's Urban Ed

http://eric-web.tc.columbia.edu/digests/dig126.html

This site is a clearinghouse ERIC Digest, Turning it around for all youth: from risk to resilience.

Acceptable Use Policies

http://chico.rice.edu/armadillo/Rice/Resources/
acceptable.html

Many schools which provide Internet access to students and staff have created policies and agreements for the appropriate use of Internet accounts. Samples of agreements, policies, and opinion pieces have been collected at Armadillo's World Wide Web server.

Counseling and Technology Bibliography

http://www.schoolcounselor.com/bibliogr.htm

part

2

A Tour of the World Wide Web for School Counselors

```
http://www.thejournal.com/magazine/vault/
A1914.cfm
```

World School Directory

```
http://www.education-world.com/regional/k12_schools
```

This site is a country-by-country and state-by-state guide to K12 Schools, Universities, and Education Resources around the world. Users can find the following LOCAL Schools within this guide:

- Charter Schools & School Districts
- Montessori Schools
- Parochial Schools & School Districts
- Private Schools
- Public Schools & School Districts
- Gifted and Talented School Districts
- Special Needs School Districts
- Universities & University Departments

Also available are the following related resources:

- Education Organizations
- K12 School Libraries
- School Newspapers
- K12 School Publications
- Alumni Publications
- Regional Education Resources
- Vocational—Technical Schools
- Gifted and Talented School
- International School
- Magnet Schools
- Online Schools
- Special Needs Schools

Goals 2000

```
http://www.ed.gov/pubs/G2KReforming
```

Goals 2000: Reforming Education to Improve Student Achievement (April 1998) looks at how Goals 2000 supports state efforts to develop clear and rigorous standards for what every child should know and be able to do, and supports comprehensive state- and district-wide planning and implementation of school efforts focused on improving student achievement of those standards.

part
2

ASCD Education Bulletin

Email: Bulletin@listserv.ascd.org

This biweekly online newsletter of the Association for Supervision and Curriculum Development (ASCD) International is dedicated to sharing and exchanging information on the issues of international development, democracy, and professional development.

American School Counselors Association Materials

http://www.schoolcounselor.org.

ASCA has also developed national standards for school counselors. Descriptions of the duties and goals of school counselors are listed. Copies are available on their Web site along with *Get a Life Portfolio* (in single or bulk rates):

- *Facilitator's Manual*—eight chapters of practical information and in-service activities for local staff and community helpers (131 pages).
- *Facilitator's Guide*—5-page quick-reference guide to help teachers and advisors maximize the *Get A Life Portfolio*.
- *Introductory Video* (10 minutes)—introduces the program to school staff, parents, and community groups.
- *Get A Life Software*—storage, retrieval, and editing software to help track student goals (DOS compatible, 3–½" disks).
- *Macintosh Programming Guide*—for customizing the program and creating word processing files on a Macintosh computer.

part

2

Keeping Track of Time for School Counselors

http://www.hotfiles.com

This is a great share/freeware spot on the Web for personal information managers. Uses could include a database to simplify the school counselor's job of keeping track of time.

School Counselor Web Link

http://www.uncg.edu/edu/ericcass/libhome.htm

This site has links to numerous articles and resources for school counselors. Issues covered relate to bullying, substance abuse, violence, suicide, gangs, career development, student achievement, cultural diversity, conflict resolution, and the list goes on and on.

Transitioning

http://www.middleweb.com/INCASE5to6.html

A collection of good ideas for fifth–sixth grade transitioning.

Books for Middle School

All of the following are available from www. amazon.com

- *Enjoy Your Middle Schooler: A Guide to Understanding the Physical, Social, Emotional, and Spiritual Changes of Your eleven-to fourteen-Year-Old,* by Wayne Rice.
- *Middle School Blues,* by Lou Kassem.
- *The Middle School Maze,* by Cliff Schimmels.
- *The Parents' Public School Handbook: How to Make the Most of Your Child's Education, from Kindergarten Through Middle School,* by Kenneth Shore.

part 2

ACPS Middle Schools 24

http://www.psy.miami.edu/faculty/DGreenfield/research.html

This Web site displays a suggested time line for preschool to early elementary school transition.

Transition and Continuity between Head Start and Public Schools

http://www.acps.k12.va.us/sitemap.html

This site includes benefits of transition, keys to successful transition key concepts about transition to kindergarten, a transition checklist, differences between early childhood and kindergarten, and a kindergarten observer's worksheet.

Behavioral Interventions

Email: vstanhope@naspweb.org

The newly released publication from the Center, *Behavioral Interventions: Creating a Safe Environment in Our Schools* discusses behavioral problems in children, highlighting positive strategies and interventions. To request a free copy of *Behavioral Interventions,* email Victoria Stanhope at vstanhope@naspweb.org and give your regular mailing address.

Communities That Care

http://www.cisnet.org
http://www.americaspromise.org

For information on how to become one of Colin Powell's Schools of Promise, visit this Web site or that of Communities in Schools.

Leo Ussak Elementary School-Partners

http://www.arctic.ca/LUS/Partners.html

This page shows the multitude of community businesses and other partnerships that the Leo Ussak Elementary School in Rankin Inlet, Canada, persuaded to help them establish an Internet connection to the world, as William Belsey describes in the EL article, *Igalaaq: Window to the World.*

part 2

Dynotech Software

http://www.dyno1.com

This site provides educational software to help children with learning disabilities. Many programs are what is known as shareware or try-before-you-buy, which can be downloaded at no cost. If the user wants to continue using the software after reviewing it, he or she can pay the author's fees.

Learning Style Inventory

http://www.hcc.hawaii.edu/intranet/committees/
FacDevCom/guidebk/teachtip/lernstyl.htm

Twenty-four item learning style online survey. An evaluation tool to assess learning styles. Identifies visual/auditory/tactile learners and gives a description of each style.

K–12 Practitioners Home Page—NCES

`http://nces.ed.gov/practitioners`

The National Center for Education Statistics (NCES) has launched a site for K–12 practitioners that summarizes and explains some of the latest educational research findings. Survey data that support these findings, as well as methods used to conduct the surveys are outlined. Teachers, administrators, school support staff, and parents can examine articles in the Research Findings section on topics such as Teacher Job Satisfaction, At-Risk Students, and the Pipeline to Higher Education. Links to additional NCES resources and organizations affiliated with NCES projects are also included.

Idea Book

`http://www.ed.gov/pubs/Idea_Planning`

Implementing Schoolwide Programs: An Idea Book on Planning presents methods and resources for planning schoolwide programs and for measuring their success. It also focuses on the fact that schoolwide programs have the flexibility to combine many federal education funds with state and local funds to operate. Featured are schools that have a record of improving student performance; cohesive planning; a comprehensive, standards-based curriculum; highly qualified staff who are committed to building a culture of learning; family, school, and community partnerships that have helped sustain the school's academic achievements and have combined Title I funds with state and local resources.

Simulation Games

`http://home.pix.za/gc/gc12/simgames/simgame01.htm`

BaFa BaFa (racism and culture) is a simulation game that aims to let groups experience racist feelings toward each other, based on two hypothetical "cultures." In debriefing they will realize how racism can be based on misinformation and wrong perceptions, as well as understand how interaction can help overcome racial barriers. This can also be adapted to highlight communication between any two groups, such as parents-teens, different language groups, and different schools.

part
2

Education World®

http://www.education-world.com
http://www.education-world.com/a_curr/curr125.shtml

This site where educators go to learn is a database of over 110,000 sites featuring what's new, education topics, guide site reviews, world resource center, world school directory, cool schools, employment listings, events calendar, distribution lists, message boards, questionnaire, and awards and accolades.

7 Habits

http://www.usaweekend.com/99_issues/990124/
990124coveyhour.html

Let the *7 Habits* author and *USA Weekend* contributing editor show you how to better realize life goals with quizzes and articles at the Stephen Covey Archive.

School Psychology Resource Online

http://mail.bcpl.lib.md.us/~sandyste/p~04.html#list

This is an online resource for the school psychology community. Information on learning disabilities, ADHD, gifted, autism, adolescence, parenting, and assessment are just a few of the many resources offered.

Global School Psychologist Network

http://www.dac.neu.edu/cp/consult/

This site is moderated by Dr. L. Kruger.

Study Guides

http://www.iss.stthomas.edu/studyguides

Study Guides includes over fifty pages of summary guides to assist students in succeeding in their studies. Topics include time and stress management, test preparation, organizational strategies, reading and writing, and more. Translated into Arabic, Russian, Chinese, French, German, and Italian, the site should help students around the world. Grade level: high school. College content area: education (teaching and learning). Application type: resource.

part
2

Consortium for School Networking (CoSN)

http://www.cosn.org

Certified Cognitive-Behavioral School Counselor

http://www.nacbt.org

For a grandfathering application, call 1-800-853-1135 or email with your name and street address to nacbt@nacbt.org.

Icebreakers and Energizers

http://www.angelfire.com/ks/teachme/
icebreakers.html

This site includes some of the traditional ideas such as "people bingo" but has others as well.

part
2

Teaching Young Children How to Visualize

ASCD Education Bulletin

The biweekly online newsletter of the Association for Supervision and Curriculum Development. To subscribe:

Email:
To: BULLETIN@LISTSERV. ASCD. ORG
Subject: ASCD Education Bulletin

Nicenet

http://www.nicenet.org

Nicenet is a way for educators to set up a Web page without having to format anything. Type in the information. Try setting up a temporary account so you can view its features.

Teacher/Advisor Site

http://www.mentors.ca

This site includes an annotated bibiography that is searchable and contains virtually every published article about the Teacher–Advisor system. Seminars are provided on establishing such systems, and the Web site includes details about that curriculum as well.

Peer Counseling/Mentoring/Helping Sites

http://www.islandnet.com/~rcarr
http://www.tunnecliffe.com.au/articles.html
http://www.peerhelping.org

Research Papers

http://www.peer.ca/Docs.html.
Read one of the papers available online or access all the published
literature about peer mediation.

School Psychology Resources Online

http://mail.bcpl.lib.md.us/~sandyste

Student Counseling Centers on the Internet

http://ub-counseling.buffalo.edu

WCN (Interactive Counseling Community)

http://www.CounselingNetwork.com

part

2

Sexual Harrassment Site

http://www.schoolcounselor.com/harass.htm

Confronting Sexual Harassment: Learning Activities for Teens

http://www.educationalmedia.com/bookfiles/
confsexualharas.html

Help your teenagers develop positive personal relationships and confront
the troublesome area of sexual harassment. Eight group sessions and
twenty-seven supplementary activities are provided to challenge students
from ages twelve to eighteen to take more responsibility in creating a
safe and productive school environment. Included are reproducible
activity sheets and assessment instruments. Use with individuals, small
groups, classrooms, or community groups by Russell A. Sabella and
Robert D. Myrick, Ph.D.

COUNSELING SPECIAL CLIENT POPULATIONS

Annotated Guide to a Parent's Research for Gifted Children

http://www.hollingworth.org/cheetah.html

Is It A Cheetah? by Stephanie Tolan. This essay uses the analogy of identifying, classifying, and caging a cheetah to address some of the problems associated with raising, teaching, or being a gifted child. Good light reading.

http://www.nexus.edu.au/teachstud/gat/evanss.htm

Acceleration: A Legitimate Means of Meeting the Needs of Gifted Children, by Dr. Sarah Evans. The "best of the bunch," this critical review of accelerative methods and motivations thoroughly examines arguments both for and against acceleration in all its forms.

http://www.nexus.edu.au/teachstud/gat/evanss.htm

part **2**

The Maturity Post, by Trindel Maine (private correspondence). In examining the issue of gifted children's maturity and classroom behavior, Maine proposes an experiment: take thirty 3rd-graders and place them in 1st and 2nd grade classes, then ask, "Who is immature?"

http://www.cec.sped.org/digests/e526.htm

Should Gifted Children be Grade-Advanced? by Sharon Lynch. According to this review of current research, the majority of studies have shown that children who have been academically accelerated do not suffer academically or socially.

http://www.gifteddevelopment.com/
Whatwe'velearned.html

What We Have Learned About Gifted Children, by Linda Silverman. Key findings indicate that gifted children need different teaching methods from non-gifted learners, and that gifted children have better social adjustment in classes with children like themselves, whether age-peer gifted or intellectual peers.

http://www.edweek.org/ew/vol-16/07winner.h16

The Miseducation of Our Gifted Children, by Ellen Winner, in *Education Week.* Providing special education to gifted children offends our egalitarian sensibilities, but we need to recognize the importance of appropriate education techniques to teaching gifted children.

http://www.hoagiesgifted.org/

Struggle, Challenge, and Meaning: The Education of a Gifted Child, by Valerie Bock. Gifted children deserve the same opportunities as other children to test their mettle and emerge victorious, and to experience the rewards of meaningful work.

http://www.hoagiesgifted.org/

Horizontal Enrichment versus Vertical Acceleration, by Draper Kauffman, Ed. D. Items with standard 2nd grade vocabulary and standard explanations are unlikely to interest a gifted 2nd grader.

http://www.hoagiesgifted.org/

Parents Wish List for Educators, Jean Schweers, Ed.D. "We, the parents of gifted and talented students, wish schools, administrators, and teachers would. . . ."

Hoagies' Gifted Education Page

http://www.hoagiesgifted.org/

This extensive site helps meet the needs of parents and educators of gifted children. Included are articles, research, books, organizations, conferences, online support groups, academic programs, products, and organizations that support gifted education locally, nationally, and globally.

Exceptional Education Federal Regulations

http://www.ideapractices.org/finalregs.htm

This site posts newly released federal regulations for exceptional children.

Selective Mutism

http://www.lib.muohio.edu/edpsych/wwwboard/
messages/17.html

http://www.anxietynetwork.com/spsm.html

Anxiety Disorders Association of America

http://www.adaa.org

part
2

Association for the Advancement of Behavior Therapy

http://server.psyc.vt.edu/aabt

Selective Mutism Foundation

http://personal.mia.bellsouth.net/mia/g/a/garden/
garden/home.htm

Family Village Selective Mutism Page

http://laran.waisman.wisc.edu/fv/www/
lib_selmutism.htm

Suite 101: Lisa Hogan's Special Education Site

http://www.suite101.com/welcome.cfm/
special_education

This site rates the top five Web sites for special education. It also contains current featured articles and links for parents with children in special education.

American Association of Mental Retardation

http://www.aamr.org/index.html

This is an online resource for publications, training, careers, conventions, policies, and resources.

Bureau for At Risk Youth

http://www.at-risk.com

This is a resource site to help today's youth cope with important issues that face them. It includes an at risk resources directory, an issues forum, a buyer's guide, and a free catalogue order form.

Psychotherapy Library

http://www.psychotherapylibrary.com/

DRuG EDucation ReSourCes

http://hometown.aol.com/drgedrscs/index.htm

part
2

This web site contains search engines and links for definitions, statistics, facts, and useful tools for drug free programs, natural highs and relaxation programs.

At-Risk Directed Research and Publications

http://www.ed.gov/offices/OERI/At-Risk/direct1.html

This site outlines successful at-risk programs.

ADHD/ADD Regulation Site

http://www.ed.gov/offices/OSERS/IDEA/Brief-6.html

This is a Web site that offers access to federal regulations online via GPO access. It contains a browse feature and also contains final regulations on Brief 6 for children with ADD/ADHD— March 1999.

ADD Assessment

http://www.amenclinic.com,

Dr. Daniel Amen has a fascinating Web site that has a huge source of resources related to ADD/ADHD. One of his books, *Windows Into the ADD Mind,* is great reading for someone interested in the subject.

Children and Adults with Attention Deficit Disorder (CHADD)

http://www.chadd.com

ADD Newsletter

http://www.helpforadd.com

In addition to this site, David Rabiner also publishes an online newsletter entitled *ADHD research update.* There is a modest cost for the online research newsletter however David offers free issues for review.

The ADD/ADHD/LD Links and Resources Page

http://www.angelfire.com/ny/Debsimms/add.html

ADD Main Table of Contents

http://www3.sympatico.ca/frankk/contents.html

part

2

Fifty Tips on the Classroom Management of Attention Deficit Disorder

http://www3.sympatico.ca/frankk/50class.html

LD in Depth: ADD/ADHD Resources

http://www.ldonline.org/ld_indepth/add_adhd/
add-adhd.html

Attention Deficit Disorder in the Classroom

http://www.chadd.org/fact4.htm

National Attention Deficit Disorder Association

http://www.add.org./

ADD Warehouse

http://www.addwarehouse.com

1-800-233-9273

Related Sites:

http://www.sciam.com/1998/0998issue/0998barkley.html

http://www.mentalhealth.com/dis-rs/frs-ch01.html

ADDHELP-Attention Deficit Disorder-Solutions for Teachers and Parents of ADD/ADHD Kids

http://www.addhelp.com/home.html

This site has a lot of great tips as well as information about how to order a really good book on the subject.

ADD/Parent Site

http://www.med.virginia.edu/medicine/clinical/pediatr
ics/devbeh/adhdlin/

This site was created by a teacher who has an ADD-ADHD child. There is a lot of information on this site and is very well worth the time it will take to look it over.

ADHD / Special Needs Resources: Kids Who Thrive "Outside the Box!"

http://home.att.net/~shagberg/

Grade Level: K–12, Parent & Professional

Teaching Tips: ADHD

http://www.central.edu/education/REX/adhd.html

This site includes helpful information for dealing with the ADHD student in your classroom, including good teaching tips and strategies for the teacher.

Adults with Attention Deficit Disorder

Email: adult@maelstrom.stjohns.edu

http://yourhealthdaily.com	Daily Health News
http://tristate.pgh.net/~pinch13	Outstanding Kid's Resource Page
http://members.aol.com/nfgcc	(National Foundation for Gifted and Creative Children)
http://www.studentservices.com/fastweb/	Financial Aid Scholarship Search
http://www.petersons.com/	College Applications
http://family.starwave.com/funstuff/	Family Activities
http://www.ed.gov/pubs/parents.html	Government Education Publications
http://trace.wisc.edu/gofr_web/handbook	Download ADA Handbook
ADA-related Information	800–669-EEOC
ADD-ONS	P. O. Box 675, Frankfort, IL 60423
ADDA	800-487-2282
ADDult News	2620 Ivy Place, Toledo, OH 43613
ADDvantage	P.O. Box 29972, Thornton, CO 80229
Advocacy, Incorporated	800-252-9108
Ch.A.D.D.	800-233-4050
Challenge, Incorporated	P.O. Box 488, West Newbury, MA 01985
Learning Disabilities Association	412-340-1515
National Center For Law and Learnng Disabilities, Incorporated	301-469-8308

part

2

ACT Web Site–Information for Life's Transitions

http://www.act.org

Closed Captioning Web

http://www.users.erols.com/berke

This site has information accessible to students with hearing impairments, ESL, and other language difficulties. Links to companies that provide nonprofessional captioning software are available so that, for a relatively small fee, counselors can caption their own educational materials.

Disability Information and Resources

http://www.eskimo.com/~jlubin/disabled.html

A directory of many disability resources. This site contains links to general disability resources, newsletters, Web sites on people with disabilities, a disability-solutions page, and current political stances of disability.

Dyslexia

http://www.dyslexia.com

The Gift is an online information center dedicated to the positive side of learning disability as well as to remedial therapies and teaching methods suited to the dyslexic learning style.

Internet Resources for Special Children

http://www.irsc.org

Information for parents, educators, medical professionals, and others who interact with children who have disabilities.

MedWeb

http://www.medweb.emory.edu/medweb/default.htm

Contains links to an array of disability-related information.

Organizations and Associations Worldwide for Down Syndrome

http://www.nas.com/downsyn/org.html

Includes contact information and links, when available, to worldwide associations for Down Syndrome.

Parent Soup

http://www.parentsoup.com/edcentral/LD

Parent Soup is a parenting library about learning disabilities and dyslexia. It contains articles ranging from memory problems to treatment.

Recording for the Blind and Dyslexic (RFB&D)

http://www.rfbd.org

A national nonprofit organization that serves people who cannot read standard print because of a visual, perceptual, or other physical disability. The organization also offers the nonprofit sale of dictionaries, reference materials, and professional books on computer disk (E-text), and specially adapted tape players/recorders to use with their audio books.

The Sibling Support Project Home Page

http://www.chmc.org/departmt/sibsupp

Dedicated to the interests of brothers and sisters of people with special health and developmental needs, this site offers information about workshops, existing sibling programs, resources, and SibNet (a list service for siblings of people with special needs.

National Academy for Child Development (NACD)

http://www.nacd.org

An international organization of parents and professionals dedicated to helping children and adults reach their full potential, NACD designs very specific home educational and therapeutic programs for infants, children, and adults.

The James Stanfield Publishing Company

http://www.stanfield.com

The most respected library of educational materials available today for students with cognitive challenges, the company provides texts for programs about assertion training, sexuality education, social skills, and working skills.

part
2

UPSIDE!

http://www.telebyte.com/upside/upside.html

National Organization of Rare Disorders, Inc. (NORD)

http://www.pcnet.com/~orphan/welcome.htm

NORD is a federation of more than 140 not-for-profit volunteer health organizations serving people with rare disorders and disabilities.

Kids Together, Inc.

http://www.kidstogether.org

The mission statement of this nonprofit organization is "To promote inclusive communities where all people belong." The site provides helpful information and resources to enhance the quality of life for children and adults with disabilites, and for communities. Businesses can take advantage of the numerous marketing opportunities offered by the Kids Together Day Festival.

Multicultural Discovery Activities for the Elementary Grades

By Elizabeth Stull. Contains 150 reproducible pages addressing a variety of cultures. MarCo Products 1–800–448–2197

The School Counselor's Book of Lists

1–800–288–4745. Ask for title code C1293–4.

Bullying Online

http://www.successunlimited.co.uk
http://www.successunlimited.co.uk/child.htm

More Bullying Sites

http://trms.k12.ga.net/~abaggett/center.html
http://www.esu3.org/web/mscc.html
http://www.wwwcomm.com/guidance

Healthy Oakland Teens Curriculum

http://www.caps.ucsf.edu/curricula/hotcurr.html

The Healthy Oakland Teens curriculum is divided into six teacher-led sessions and eight peer-led sessions available for download.

Electronic Schoolhouse

http://edweb.gsn.org
http://teachnet.com

Suicide Resources for Teachers

http://www.himh.org.au/Origin.html

Employers, Families, and Education

http://www.ed.gov/pubs/EmpFamEd

This site tells how employers can improve education through family-friendly business policies and partnerships with local schools. *The Corporative Imperative: Results and Benefits of Business Involvement in Education* explores how businesses can create strategic education alliances that meet business objectives and promote systemic education change.

ASSESSMENT AND TESTING RESOURCES

Consulting Psychologists Press, Inc.

http://www.cpp-db.com/

CPP is the exclusive publisher of the Myers-Briggs Type Indicator. (MBTI), Strong Interest InventoryTM, FIROTM, and the CPITM.

Keirsey Temperament and Character Web Site

http://www.keirsey.com

This link is for a free test that is very similar to the Myers-Briggs.

part

2

Buros Institute of Mental Measurements

http://www.unl.edu/buros

This site provides professional assistance, expertise, and information to users of commercially published tests. Listed are records of over 10,000 tests and research instruments, including information about ETS tests on microfiche. The site includes a test locator and subject index.

ERIC/AE Test Locator-Gopher

gopher://vmsgopher.cua.edu./11gopher_root_eric_ae:
[_tc]

This is an updated test locator including ERIC Clearinghouse for assessment and evaluation.

PARENT EDUCATION

part
2

U.S. Department of Education

http://www.ed.gov/pubs/parents.html

Helping Your Child Learn Math . . . Reading . . . History . . . Responsible Behavior—all these resources are online at the U.S. Department of Education, including a new report, *Simple Things You Can Do to Help a Child Read Well and Independently.*

American Library Association's site

http://www.ala.org/parentspage

Family Education Network

http://familyeducation.com/article/0,1120,
1-9834-1,00.html

Apple Learning Interchange

http://ali.apple.com/

These online handouts contain wonderful topics such as how to complain constructively, the importance of reading, parent and family places online, parents, homework, and computers, preparing your child for the first day of school, and separation anxieties.

PARENTING WORKSHOPS

The Positive Parenting Page

http://positiveparenting.com/index.html

Stephen Glenn and Jane Nelsen's work

http://www.empoweringpeople.com

For Everything on Adolescence

http://education.indiana.edu/cas/normal.html

Step Kit by Dinkmeyer

http://www.agsnet.com

The National PTA

http://www.pta.org

The National PTA has developed national standards for parent and family involvement in schools.

Parent Time

http://www.parenttime.com

Sponsored by Time Warner, this site provides multiple entry points for parents, including ways to help their children in school. Search the site for "roller coaster" and find articles full of practical advice for parents and teachers of young adolescents.

America Goes Back to School

http://www.ed.gov/Family/agbts

ICN Digest

Email: cpool@ascd.org

Web Wonders: Engaging Parents and Community in Schools, compiled by Carolyn R. Pool.

part

2

Growing Up Drug-Free: A Parent's Guide to Prevention

http://www.ed.gov/offices/OESE/SDFS/parents_guide

This site includes suggestions on talking with your children effectively, what to do if you think your child might be using drugs, how to teach your child about drugs, where to get information and help, and more.

The Connect for Kids Weekly

http://www.connectforkids.org

This site is a source for the latest news on issues affecting kids and families published by the Benton Foundation.

Red Ribbon Week Resource

http://www.redribboncoalition.org

Home and School Institute

http://www.MegaSkillsHSI.org

How do parents rate the teachers of their children? What can schools and teachers learn from parents' answers to questions like "Does this teacher appear to enjoy teaching and believe in what he or she does in school"? Dorothy Rich of the Home and School Institute explores the results of such surveys in her EL article, *What Parents Want from Teachers*.

MEDIATION RESOURCES/SAFE SCHOOLS

Conflict Resolution

http://www.bouldenpub.com

This site offers free demo conflict resolution interactive CDs to elementary school counselors. This CD runs on both Mac and PC and contains relaxation exercise plus limited demo of interactive material. If interested, send $3.75 to cover shipping to address below. email: jboulden@bouldenpub.com

A Guide to Safe Schools

http://www.ed.gov/offices/OSERS/OSEP/earlywrn.html
http://www.ed.gov/PressReleases/08-1998/violence.html

Early Warning, Timely Response: A Guide to Safe Schools was developed at the President's request by the Departments of Justice and Education, in cooperation with the National Association of School Psychologists. It tells what to look for and what to do to prevent violence, how to intervene and get help for troubled children, and how to respond when violent situations occur. (The guide is also available by calling 1–877–4ED-PUBS.)

NCES Publication Released

`http://nces.ed.gov/pubsearch`

This report, *Indicators of School Crime and Safety, 1988,* is the first in a series of annual reports on school crime and safety from the Bureau of Justice Statistics and the National Center for Education Statistics. It presents the latest available data on school crime and student safety. The report provides a profile of school crime and safety in the United States and describes the characteristics of the victims of these crimes. It is organized as a series of indicators, with each indicator presenting data on different aspects of school crime and safety. There are five sections to the report: Nonfatal Student Victimization—Student Reports; Violence and Crime at School; Nonfatal Teacher Victimization at School—Teacher Reports; and School Environment. Each section contains a set of indicators that, taken as a whole, describe a distinct aspect of school crime and safety.

part
2

Center for Prevention of School Violence

`http://www.ncsu.edu/cpsv/`

This site offers information, program assistance, and research on school violence prevention. The "Safe Schools Pyramid" offers prevention programs such as "School Resource Officers" and "Conflict Management Peer Mediation."

Teacher Talk

`http://education.indiana.edu/cas/tt/ttarticles.html`

This site focuses on ways to manage student disruptions. Under "Interventions" click on "Respect" and "Topics for Creating a Peaceful Classroom" for simple steps educators can take to ensure a friendlier and more productive relationship with students.

NEA Today Online: One Year After the School Shootings

`http://www.nea.org/neatoday`

In the year since the tragic school shootings in Arkansas, Oregon, and Pennsylvania, NEA members nationwide have been working to create schools where all students feel safe. The April edition of *NEA Today Online* synthesizes the latest research.

NEA Response to Littleton, Colorado

http://www.nea.org/nr/st990421.html

This NEA html page posts responses and recommendations for prevention of school violence after the Littleton, Colorado massacre.

Violence Prevention Resource

http://www.schoolcounselor.org.

If you click on violence prevention, then the table of contents, you will get to the pledges. There is an elementary pledge, a special edition pledge to the gorp (along with a special offer to school counselors in the books and resource section of the table of contents in this area for "the Gorps Gift"), and a pledge for older students . . . as well as the no taunting pledge from the nea and the ribbons of promise pledge.

Blueprint for Violence Prevention

http://www.colorado.edu/cspv/blueprints/index.html

This site is an excellant resource for violence prevention from the Center for the Study and Prevention of Violence (CSPV) and the Colorado Division of Criminal Justice and the Center for Disease Control (CDC). This site identifies ten violence prevention programs which meet high standards in program effectiveness. They include: Midwestern Prevention, Big Brothers—Big Sisters, Functional Family Therapy, Multisystemic Therapy, Nursing Home Visitation, Treatment Foster Care, Quantum Opportunities, Life Skills Training, Paths, and Bullying Prevention.

Association for School Curriculum Development (ASCD)

http://www.ascd.org/safeschools/

This Web site offers resources on violence prevention which includes books and articles.

Selected ERIC Abstracts on School Violence

■ *Reducing School Violence through Conflict Resolution Training*
NASSP Bulletin v80 n579 p11–18 Apr 1996

- *Taking a Stand Against Violence. Leadership and Responsibility: One School's Quest to Create a Safe Harbor*   UMI 1-800-248-0360
- *Drugs and School Violence*   Education and Treatment of Children, v20 n3 p263–80 Aug. 1997
- *The Evolution of Violence in Schools*   Educational Leadership, v55 n2 p18–20 Oct 1997
- *What is Violence Prevention, Anyway?*   Educational Leadership, v54 n8 p31–33 May 1997
- *Protecting Your School and Students: The Safe Schools Handbook*   NASSP Bulletin, v80 n579 p44–48 Apr 1996
- *The Art of Safe School Planning*   School Administrator, v53 n2 p14–21 Feb 1996
- *Safe School: A Planning Guide for Action. 1995 Edition*   California State Department of Education, Sacramento: California State Office of the Attorney General, Sacramento. 174p.: For 1989 edition, see ED 313 815
- *A Guide to Violence Prevention*   Educational Leadership, v52 n5 p57–59 Feb 1995
- *Real School Safety Depends upon Safe-Oriented Discipline Policies*   EDRS 1–800–443–3742 Ref #ED330028
- *How to Keep Your School and Students Safe. Tips for Principals from NASSP*   National Association of Secondary School Principals, Reston, Va. (703–684–3345) Mar 1990 3p.
- *A Study of the Knowledge and Skills of Teachers on School Safety*   Nov. 1996 13p.; Paper presented at the Mid-South Education Research Association (Tuscaloosa, AL., November 6, 1996). EDRS 1–800–443–3742 Ref ED402296
- *In Pursuit of Goal Six: A Statewide Initiative to Improve School Safety*   Apr 1994 18p.; Paper presented at the Annual Meeting of the American Educational Research Association (New Orleans, LA, April 4–8, 1994). EDRS 1-800-443-3742 Ref #373453

part

2

HOMESCHOOLING

Jon's Homeschool Resources Page

http://www.midnightbeach.com/hs/Welcome.html

Jon Shemitz keeps his site up-to-date with a variety of resources for homeschoolers, including links to listservs, discussion groups, Web sites, and local and national support groups. The site also contains some full-text articles.

Homeschool Headlines

`http://www.homeschoolheadlines.com`

A free online publication to support, inform, and empower homeschoolers, this site offers many articles. Some articles offer practical advice about teaching math; others tell success stories. Click on "Controversial Issues" for differing views on the questions: Should There Be a Separation Between School and State? or Should Government Continue Directing Education in America? The site also includes newsletters aimed at homeschoolers in Maryland and Pennsylvania.

The Wonderful WWW Page of Homeschooling Humor

`http://users.aol.com/WERHSFAM/humor.html`

Click on the top ten lists for a laugh and to see if you recognize yourself in any of them. This page also features a long list of links. Visit one link, the "School Is Dead; Learn in Freedom!" page, (http://learninfreedom.org/), and click on "About" for exceptionally useful notes on how to build a Web page.

Colleges That Admit Homeschoolers FAQ

`http://learninfreedom.org/colleges_4_hmsc.html`

Here's another page from "School Is Dead; Learn in Freedom!" You've homeschooled your kids and now it's time to think about applying to college. This site lists more than 730 links to colleges and universities that have accepted homeschooled students. Scroll through the list to find information and resources from universities, homeschooling associations, and government agencies.

Manitoba Homeschool Page

`http://www.flora.org/homeschool-ca/test/index.htm`

Canadians (and others) can try this page, which has the province's rules and regulations for home-based educators, a registration page for "homeschool keypals," a great annotated list of Internet links (including sites originating in the Netherlands and the United Kingdom), and a great quote from Mark Twain: "Don't let school interfere with your education." (This quote itself is also a link to Twain e-texts, including *Huckleberry Finn* and *A Connecticut Yankee*.)

The National Homeschool Association

http://www.n-h-a.org

Based in the United States, this association's site isn't very interactive, but it provides basic information about the association's mission, philosophy, and offerings. An address and telephone number are listed for further details.

Calvert School

http://www.calvertschool.org/hid.htm

An accredited home instruction source long used by United States foreign service personnel, missionaries, and other folks stationed in remote places, this nonprofit organization offers a full nondenominational, nonsectarian curriculum for K-8 students, including advisory teachers, chat rooms, electronic bulletin boards, CD-ROMs, and multimedia resources.

part
2

Biblical Foundations for Christian Homeschooling

http://pages.prodigy.com/christianhmsc/home.htm

By far, the most prominent feature of homeschooling Web sites researched is the Christian faith. The Moore family has created this site to encourage other Christian homeschooling families. Read Robert Moore's *A Philosophy for Christian Education* and *Quiet Time—Or How To Survive Your First Year Of Homeschooling*.

Rescue 2010

http://www.nace-cee.org/rescue2010.htm

Rescue 2010 is a movement that endorses homeschooling for Christian families and promotes seeking "common ground" on controversial issues; seeking "safe-passage" for all K-12 children throughout the system by being spiritually and morally unharmed or academically stunted; and organizing Christians in every school district to become involved in their local schools to oversee and ensure the above objectives.

Islamic Educational and Muslim Home School Resources

`http://home.ici.net/~taadah/taadah.html`

Not just the Christian faith is represented in the homeschooling community. This page offers teaching ideas for Muslims and non-Muslims, lists curriculum resources, and sponsors a listserv for all Muslim educators.

SCHOOL COUNSELING JOURNALS

The Journal of Technology in Counseling

`http://jtc.colstate.edu`

A peer reviewed journal, soon to be published quarterly (July, October, January, and April) through the efforts of the Department of Counseling and Clinical Programs at Columbus State University. JTC is published in a Web-based format and represents an innovative approach to publication not seen in the counseling literature. Submissions will be accepted effective April 1, 1999. *The Journal of Technology in Counseling* publishes articles on all aspects of practice, theory, research, and professionalism related to the use of technology in counselor training and counseling practice. For more information about the journal take a look at the JTC Web site which contains a list of current journal editors, guidelines for authors, and a sample design format to assist authors.

Mediation Quarterly

`http://www.jbp.com/JBJournals/mq.html`

Counselor Education and Supervision

`http://www.counseling.org/journals/ces.htm`

Elementary School Guidance and Counseling

`http://www.counseling.org/journals/subscriptions.`
`htm#Elementary`

Journal of Humanistic Education and Development

`http://www.counseling.org/journals/jhead.htm`

Journal of Special Education Technology

`http://monster.educ.kent.edu/deafed/ivc37.htm`

part
2

AIDS Education and Prevention

http://www.guilford.com/periodicals/jnai.htm

Journal of HIV/AIDS Prevention and Education for Adolescents and Children

http://web.spectra.net/cgi-bin/haworth/
j-title_search?SearchTitle=Journal%20of%20HIV

TECHNOLOGY RESOURCES

ERIC Digest

http://www.ed.gov/databases/ERIC_Digests/ed347480.html

For ideas on using computers with elementary kids, "Counseling Using Technology with At-Risk Youth" is available free online. The ERIC reference number is ED347480, Dec. '92.

Developmental Issues for School Counselors Using Technology

part 2

http://www.schoolcounselor.org

A special issue edited by Ed Gerler, devoted to "Special Edition on Applications of Computer Technology," has a number articles of related interest for elementary counseling applications.

Counseling and Technology Bibliography

http://www.schoolcounselor.com/bibliogr.htm

Tools for Schools; Families and Schools Together

http://www.ed.gov/pubs/ToolsforSchools/fast.html

Addictions/Dual Diagnosis

SUBSTANCE ABUSE

Substance Abuse and Treatment of State and Federal Prisoners

http://www.ojp.usdoj.gov/bjs/abstract/satsfp97.htm

Released on January 5, this new study by the Bureau of Justice Statistics (BJS) reports a rise in the proportion of state inmates who used drugs (including alcohol) in the month before their arrest and an increase in the use by federal inmates within prisons between 1990 and 1997. In the same period, the proportions of state inmates receiving drug abuse treatment fell from 24.5 percent in 1991 to 9.7 percent in 1997, and the numbers of inmates in treatment in federal prisons fell from 15.7 percent to 9.2 percent. Analysts attribute these figures to both a new awareness by police and the court system toward offender drug use and the exploding prison population, which has doubled since it reached 1.8 million in 1981. Available in .pdf or ASCII format, the report contains data tables on "prior alcohol and drug abuse by types of offender characteristics," as well as the types of treatment and programs in prisons. A press release, spreadsheets in .zip format, and related data sets are also available.

College on Problems of Drug Dependence (CPDD)

http://views.vcu.edu/cpdd

CPDD serves as an interface among governmental, industrial, and academic communities maintaining liaisons with regulatory and research agencies as well as educational, treatment, and prevention facilities in the drug abuse field. It also functions as a collaborating center of the World Health Organization.

Drug Strategies

http://www.drugstrategies.org

Drug Strategies is a nonprofit research institute promoting more effective approaches to the nation's drug problems by supporting private and public initiatives that reduce the demand for drugs through prevention, education, treatment, law enforcement, and community coalitions.

Center for Education and Drug Abuse Research (CEDAR)

http://www.pitt.edu/~cedar

CEDAR serves to elucidate the factors contributing to the variation in the liability to drug abuse and determine the developmental pathways culminating in drug abuse outcome, normal outcome, and psychiatric/behavioral disorder outcome. CEDAR is a consortium between the University of Pittsburgh and St. Francis Medical Center.

part
2

The American Council for Drug Education

http://www.drughelp.org

This site contains information on drugs and other harmful substances and contains a database of more then 1,200 treatment programs. It also covers topics like alcohol in the workplace, drugs and pregnancy, and talking to a child about marijuana.

International Narcotics Research Conference (INRC)

http://osu.com.okstate.edu/inrc/index.htm

Now in its 29th year, the International Narcotics Research Conference is an annual meeting designed to bring together drug abuse researchers from around the world. A diverse group of scientists present their latest results on the basic mechanisms of narcotic drug action. Important advances in molecular, cellular, and behavioral aspects of narcotic action are presented and discussed. Attendance is open and further information can be obtained from:

part

2

The National Center on Addiction and Substance Abuse at Columbia University (CASA)

http://www.casacolumbia.org

The National Center on Addiction and Substance Abuse at Columbia University (CASA) is a resource for research on addiction and substance abuse. It provides access to information, research, and commentary on tobacco, alcohol, and drug abuse issues including prevention, treatment, and cost data.

National Clearinghouse for Drug and Alcohol Information/Prevention Online

http://www.health.org
http://www.health.org/resref.htm

The National Clearinghouse for Alcohol and Drug Information (NCADI) is the information service of the Center for Substance Abuse Prevention of the U.S. Department of Health and Human Services. NCADI is the world's largest resource for current information and materials about alcohol and other drugs. The National Clearinghouse for Alcohol and Drug Information is a site which contains: missing children links, funding opportunities, treatment organizations, information on federal workplace, drug testing programs, laboratories for urine drug testing, resource for runaways, Internet links, and publications from NCADI. This Web site contains links to other Internet sites related to substance abuse information.

National Association of Alcoholism and Drug Abuse Counselors

http://www.naadac.org

NAADAC's mission is to provide leadership in the alcoholism and drug abuse counseling profession by building new visions, effecting change in public policy, promoting criteria for effective treatment, encouraging adherence to ethical standards, and ensuring professional growth for alcoholism and drug abuse counselors.

The Office of National Drug Control Policy

http://www.ncjrs.org/htm/toc.htm

The Office of National Drug Control Policy (ONDCP) was established by Act of Congress in 1988 and is organized within the Executive Office of the President. ONDCP is authorized to develop and coordinate the policies, goals, and objectives of the nation's drug control program for reducing the use of illicit drugs. ONDCP engages in activities that both meet the requirements of its authorization and represent the values and commitments of the President and its Director.

Robert Wood Johnson Foundation Substance Abuse Policy Research Program

http://www.phs.bgsm.edu/sshp/rwj/rwj.htm

The site includes project summaries, grant application information, and links to other sites relating to substance abuse. The goal of the program is to identify, analyze, and evaluate policies regarding tobacco, alcohol, and drug abuse.

The Substance Abuse and Mental Health Data Archive (SAMHDA)

http://www.icpsr.umich.edu/SAMHDA

SAMHDA's purpose is to increase the utilization of substance abuse and mental health databases, thereby encouraging their use to understand and assess the extent of alcohol, drug abuse, and mental health disorders, and the nature and impact of related treatment systems. Based at the University of Michigan's Inter-university Consortium for Political and Social Research (ICPSR).

The UCLA Drug Abuse Research Center (DARC)

http://www.medsch.ucla.edu/som/npi/DARC/search.html

The Drug Abuse Research Center (DARC) is a diverse research organization that investigates psychosocial and epidemiological issues pertaining to drug use and conducts evaluations of interventions for drug dependence. The group's portfolio of studies has provided findings that have improved the understanding of the complex nature of drug use and dependence. DARC findings have been useful in developing more effective strategies for dealing with drug-related problems through prevention, treatment, and criminal justice approaches.

Web of Addictions

http://www.well.com/user/woa

The Web of Addictions is dedicated to providing accurate information about alcohol and other drug addictions. The Web of Addictions was developed for several reasons: concern about the pro drug use messages in some Web sites and in some use groups; concern about the appalling extent of misinformation about abused drugs on the Internet, particularly on some usenet news groups; and the desire to provide a resource for teachers, students, and others who need factual information about abused drugs.

National Institute on Drug Abuse (NIDA)

http://www.nida.nih.gov

This Web site contains recent studies funded by NIDA, research on tobacco, research on economic costs of alcohol and drug abuse in the United States, latest survey results, research reports on addiction, NIDA information fax, a bi-monthly newsletter, materials for teachers, scientists, health practitioners, and students, subscription to mailing lists, science drug education, constituent organizations, grantees, government sites of interest, and site searches.

http://www.nida.nih.gov/Prevention/Prevopen.html

The government has officially embraced a new approach to drug abuse, emphasizing both counseling and medical treatment of addiction. The

part

2

National Institute on Drug Abuse issued two treatment manuals that take counselors and other professionals step-by-step through a drug treatment program. "For the first time the strategy is what I feel to be a science-based strategy," NIDA director Dr. Alan Leshner told a conference of drug abuse professionals.

Children of Alcoholics

http://www.hazelden.org

The Recovery Net

http://members.aol.com/r2135/index.htm

The Recovery Network, an organization whose mission is to provide "prevention and recovery information, interaction and support concerning substance use and abuse, addiction to alcohol, tobacco and other drugs, and behavioral and mental health problems," maintains this site which digests the latest news from over 1,400 sources (according to site). At this time, *Recovery Network News* contains approximately one week's worth of article digests from such sources as the *Wall Street Journal, USA Today,* the *Washington Post, Reuters,* the *New York Times,* and *Investors Business Daily.* The news can be downloaded as a Microsoft Word file, and interested readers can also subscribe to a weekly email version.

Center on Substance Abuse for Teens

http://www.wholefamily.com/kidteencenter/thecenter.html

Check out the fantastic new Substance Abuse Center.

Manual of Therapeutics for Addictions

http://www.wiley.com/psychiatry/miller.htm

A practical guide to the effective diagnosis and treatment of alcohol and drug addictive disorders. Edited by Norman Miller, University of Illinois, Mark S. Gold, University of Florida, and David E. Smith, American Society of Addiction Medicine.

Collegiate Alcohol and Other Drug Use

http://www.lasalle.edu/~chapman

Center for Education and Drug Abuse Research (University of Pittsburgh)

http://www.pitt.edu/~cedar/

Phoenix House

http://www.phoenixhouse.org

This New York nonprofit substance abuse service organization has established a site with referral information, its treatment philosophy and other material.

Addiction Psychiatry: Current Diagnosis and Treatment

http://www.wiley.com/psychiatry/norman.htm

This site is authored by Norman S. Miller, MD, University of Illinois at Chicago.

Buprenorphine: Combating Drug Abuse with a Unique Opioid

http://www.wiley.com/psychiatry/cowan.htm

This site is edited by Alan Cowan, Temple University School of Medicine, and John W. Lewis, University of Bristol, United Kingdom.

part
2

Journal of Drug Education

http://www.baywood.com/site/new2/
viewbook.cfm?id=100132&c=

Mental Health Net

http://mentalhelp.net/guide/substnce.htm

Another Empty Bottle

http://www.alcoholismhelp.com/

For friends and family of alcoholics, this site contains links, help groups, hotlines, information, and personal stories related to alcoholism. The site features interactive chat rooms and discussion areas for individuals to share and communicate their questions and concerns. The special section For Kids is a children's complete guide to understanding alcoholism and family relations. The organized layout provides easy navigation.

Hope and Healing Web Chronicles

`http://www.hopeandhealing.com/`

Hope and Healing Web Chronicles is a healing journal focusing on the spiritual journeys and personal transformations possible for the family affected by alcoholism and addiction. The site includes insights, observations and musings of the Web publisher, W. Waldo; articles by well-known published authors; and numerous links and descriptions of Web sites related to alcoholism. This extensive site is a great place to look for support for alcoholism.

Twelve Step Cyber Cafe

`http://www.12steps.org/`

The goal of this site is to help visitors find information about addiction, as well as the help that is available. Visitors that are new to recovery might find the Menuboard of Recovery helpful. This site provides a chat room for its visitors to share their experiences with each other, and a bulletin board which provides some helpful information on local meetings throughout the world. This site is frequently updated and simple to navigate.

Common Sense

`http://www.pta.org/commonsense/`

Common Sense provides strategies for raising drug- and alcohol-free children. This site contains substance abuse prevention facts, positive parenting tips, and family prevention activities. Information is targeted toward parents of young children, but may be useful to counselors and community leaders. An informative and attractive site.

Parallel Paths of Recovery

`http://parallel-paths.virtualave.net`

Dual Diagnosis Support Group for Individuals diagnosed with a mental/emotional illness as well as an addictive disorder and their Significant Others. This site provides, email lists, chat, forums, and links for all forms of dual diagnosis.

Christians in Recovery

`http://www.christians-in-recovery.com`

Members work to regain and maintain balance and order in their lives through active discussion of the Twelve Steps, the Bible, and experiences in their own recovery. The only purpose of Christians in Recovery is to provide information and referral for anyone who desires to recover from abuse, family dysfunction, addictions of alcohol, drugs, food, and pornography. Christians in Recovery does not engage in providing individualized professional services or counseling.

Recovery Online

`http://recovery.alano.org/`

A comprehensive listing of self-help, recovery groups online, including twelve-step groups, religious groups, as well as secular groups. This is a great place to begin a search!

Al-Anon/Alateen

`http://www.Al-Anon-Alateen.org`

Al-Anon (and Alateen for younger members) is a worldwide organization that offers a self-help recovery program for families and friends of alcoholics. The listings of the Twelve Steps, Traditions, and Concepts of Al-Anon are helpful for those who are seeking more information on the goals and objectives of this program. Also included are an approved literature section, a discussion forum, and a guide for professionals.

Alcoholics Victorious

`http://av.iugm.org/`

A Christian oriented twelve-step support group for recovering alcoholics, the site includes information and referrals, literature, phone support, conferences, support group meetings, and the organization's newsletter. An informative FAQ is provided for new visitors.

Big Book of Alcoholics Anonymous

`http://www.recovery.org/aa/bigbook/ww/`

An indexed and fully searchable copy of the main text of Alcoholics Anonymous. Also online is the unpublished, original manuscript of the book.

part

2

Santa Barbara County Alchohol and Drug Program

http://www.silcom.com/~sbadp/

Connecticut Clearinghouse

http://www.ctclearinghouse.org/

Connecticut Clearinghouse is a resource center for information about alcohol, tobacco, and other drugs. A fact sheet answers many common questions in a easy-to-read manner, the research page keeps you up-to-date on certain projects, and the message page allows one to interact with others. The Connecticut Clearinghouse provides free information to Connecticut residents about chemical dependency and related topics such as mental illness, violence, fetal alcohol syndrome, and suicide.

Kathleen Sciacca

http://www.erols.com/ksciacca/

This site is designed to provide information and resources for service providers, consumers, and family members who are seeking assistance and/or education in the field of co-occurring mental illness, drug addiction and/or alcoholism in various combinations.

HabitSmart

http://www.cts.com/crash/habtsmrt/

This Web site has been constructed to provide an abundance of information about addictive behavior, including theories of habit endurance and habit change as well as tips for effectively managing problematic habitual behavior. Includes the Self-Scoring Alcohol Check-Up, an online questionnaire for people concerned about their alcohol consumption. Many of the articles are written by Robert W. Westermeyer, Ph.D.

InfoSite

http://www.drugs.indiana.edu/

An information clearinghouse of prevention, technical assistance, and information about alcohol, tobacco, and other drugs. This site includes searchable databases (including an online dictionary of street drug slang), more than 1,000 full-text documents, more than 2,000 links to prevention sites and Web pages, and a library of more than 200 educational photos of drugs available for free download. Although this site provides a great deal of information, it is not regularly updated.

Internet Alcohol Recovery Center

`http://www.med.upenn.edu/~recovery/`

This site provides information for both consumers and professionals. Highlights of this site include a chat room, information on current research, articles, and a directory of clinics/hospitals. A simple layout makes navigation easy.

Lynn's Recovery Site

`http://www.elite.net/~lcunning/`

This site is dedicated to those interested in recovery programs based on the Twelve Steps of Alcoholics Anonymous (A. A.). Since the author's personal experience is with the program of Alcoholics Anonymous, most of the material presented is based on the program of A. A. This site is frequently updated.

National Association for Christian Recovery

`http://www.christianrecovery.com/nacr.htm`

Especially helpful for clients struggling with spiritual or faith-related issues that complicate recovery, this site contains many articles, meditations, forums, and other resources, and is frequently updated.

NicNet: The Arizona Nicotine and Tobacco Network

`http://www.nicnet.org/`

A very large resource for smoking and tobacco related links. This site's library of links is divided up into 8 categories and provides many choices within each. We found it fairly easy to use, but it lacks its own content on tobacco and related topics.

Recovery Link

`http://members.aol.com/powerless/LINK.htm`

Sponsored by Friends in Recovery and Recovery Related Resources, this site is dedicated to providing a fairly comprehensive listing of alcohol

part

2

addiction related links. This site is also a large resource for testimonials from recovering alcoholics.

Secular Organizations for Sobriety

http://www.unhooked.com/

The Secular Organizations for Sobriety (SOS) is an alternative, recovery method for those alcoholics or drug addicts who are uncomfortable with the spiritual content of widely available twelve-step programs. It is a rich resource, but the home page is very busy with navigation options and graphics. A helpful FAQ answers questions in a direct manner about the organization and what it's all about.

SMART Recovery

http://www.smartrecovery.org/

SMART Recovery is an abstinence-based, not-for-profit organization with a self-help program for people having problems with drinking and using. This frequently updated site provides a broad overview of what the organization is about. It also contains several primers and manuals concerning alcoholism.

Sobriety and Recovery Resources

http://www.winternet.com/~terrym/sobriety.html

Loading time is lengthy for this huge list of resources for every aspect of recovery. Resources are organized for easy navigation.

The Royal College of Psychiatrists 'Help is at Hand' Leaflet Series University of Exeter

http://www.rcpsych.ac.uk/public/help/welcome.htm

The University of Exeter is pleased to be able to publish in full the Royal College of Psychiatrists' 'Help is at Hand' Series. The first leaflet was published seven years ago and the topics covered are continually expanding. Over four million leaflets have now been produced by the College.

Gift of Serenity

http://www.laserbuddy.com/recover/

An Al-Anon member's personal story, this site contains touching and inspiring sections on "Acceptance, Courage, Wisdom, and Hope." An

part
2

excellent resource for those who are recovering from the effects of someone else's drinking problem, this site lists links to other related sites.

Recovery Net

http://members.aol.com/r2135/

This site contains links to twelve-step programs such as Alcoholics Anonymous and to alternative programs like Rational Recovery. It is also helpful in finding discussion groups, therapists, and treatment facilities, although it needs to be updated more often.

Close to Home Online

http://www.wnet.org/closetohome/

This Web companion to the PBS program "Moyers on Addiction: Close to Home" offers more than just a synopsis of the TV series. You can find information about the effects of illegal drugs, a debate among experts about drug-related issues, advice, and listings of resources to combat illegal drug use. This site also features Overboard, a thirteen-issue soap opera comic book directed at teenagers.

part
2

AlcoWeb

http://www.alcoweb.com/

An informative site for laypeople as well as professionals, AlcoWeb's highlights include a glossary, prevention and health information, and related resources. Text is available in French and English.

My Daily Recovery

http://www.recoveryconnection.com/

My Daily Recovery is a membership-supported site which provides online services and support for individuals interested in or recovering from alcoholism, alcohol abuse, and related chemical and emotional dependencies.

Grant Me the Serenity . . .

http://www.jps.net/sunflake/

A list of recovery links, quotes, and affirmations for various forms of addiction, this site includes religious, secular, and twelve-step groups as well as links to general recovery or addiction-related sites. Resources are

organized by type of addiction with a brief description. Original graphics make this an attractive site.

Ask Dr. Steve

http://www.drsteve.org/

A thought provoking, candid assortment of facts, opinions, and
resources on all aspects of substance use and dependency. The "Ask Dr.
Steve" column is updated regularly and includes current references to
treatment methods and resources.

Recovery Network

http://www.recoverynetwork.com/

An integrated television, radio, phone, and Internet-based system
designed to deliver chemical dependency and mental health services
nation-wide via these mass communication vehicles. An interesting site,
with a great deal of potential.

Substance Abuse

http://substanceabuse.miningco.com/

With a focus on drug addiction, this site provides lots of information for
both intervention and treatment. Their frequent articles are thoughtful
and obviously well-researched. With an abound of helpful links throughout the Web page, this is a great source for information.

Dual Recovery Anonymous Twelve-Step Program

http://dualrecovery.org/dra/

This site is very comprehensive, containing twenty-one pages. Their home
page and Preamble page explain DRA's purposes, values, and philosophy.
Additional pages describe their twelve steps; their twelve traditions; answer frequently asked questions; describe their meeting formats; and list
where their groups are currently located. The site also includes a discussion forum page, a chat room, and a page set up to conduct an online
meeting. The site also includes a recovery gift shop, links to three bookstores, and search pages, for both links to other recovery sites, and other
links. Their newsletter is also available through this site. Unique links include a page linking the user to various games, and a jukebox.

part

2

Do It Now Foundation

http://www.doitnow.org/

America's drug information connection, this foundation has been developing innovative publications and education materials on substance abuse, alcoholism & related health since 1968. Currently their site archives the entire roster of educational publications in these areas. It is especially comprehensive in detailing resources about "street" drugs.

The Big Page of Information for Survivors

http://www.fiber.net/users/jeffglo/nik.htm

Contains links of interest for survivors of incest, child abuse, ritual abuse, drug addiction, and those diagnosed with Multiple Personality Disorder (Dissociation). This site was created by a survivor of sexual, emotional, physical, and ritual abuse.

ADULT CHILDREN OF ALCOHOLICS INFORMATION

Recovery.org

http://www.recovery.org/acoa/acoa.html

This site gives very basic information on adult children of alcoholics. This resource is limited, but it might be of use to point adult children of alcholics in the right direction.

Cocaine Anonymous

http://www.ca.org/

A fellowship of men and women who share their experience, strength and hope with each other so that they may solve their common problem and help others to recover from their addiction. The only requirement for membership is a desire to stop using cocaine and all other mind-altering substances. There are no dues or fees for membership.

Dave's Place

http://users.aimnet.com/~dvorous/home.html

This Web site contains information about non-twelve-step drug/alcohol recovery meetings in the San Francisco Bay Area. There is also information, including links, on various non-twelve-step recovery programs.

Readers must sift through information unrelated to substance abuse to find these resources.

Instituto para el Estudio de las Adicciones

http://www.arrakis.es/iea/

The Instituto para el Estudio de las Adicciones is an NGO located in Spain. It is the first Spanish Web site designed to prevent drug addiction. Visitors can find information about drugs, how to talk with children, a calendar of events, who is who, HIV, and more. All text is in Spanish. Loading time is lengthy.

Jewish Alcoholics, Chemically Dependent Persons and Significant Others

http://www.jacsweb.org/

An Internet recovery resource site for Jews and their families whose lives have been affected by alcohol and drugs. The site lists retreats (mostly based in the NYC area), and provides links to local support groups. Other resources are planned for this easy to navigate site.

Marijuana Anonymous

http://www.marijuana-anonymous.org/

Marijuana Anonymous is a fellowship of men and women who share the same experience of addiction. The only requirement for membership is a desire to stop using marijuana. This site contains membership information and pamphlets.

Minnesota Recovery Page

http://www.lakeweb1.com/mrp/

This site provides contact information for various twelve-step groups and recovery resources. An AA meeting directory for much of Minnesota is included.

Moderation Management

http://www.moderation.org/

A recovery program and national support group network for people who have made the healthy decision to reduce their drinking and make other positive lifestyle changes. Provides membership information, a national list of MM support groups, an MM mailing list, chat, and related literature for sale.

Narcotics Anonymous

http://www.wsoinc.com/

Provides some basic information about the Fellowship of Narcotics Anonymous. This site can be helpful in contacting with NA in or near your community.

Recovery Corner

http://www.sonic.net/~robd/recovery.html

This site is for twelve-step recovery and related topics. The main feature is the collection of message boards where individuals can post, share, and support each other.

Recovery Resources

http://www.naturesgift.com/recov.htm

This site contains many Al-Anon, AA, and other twelve-step resources. The author is in the process of recovery, and has created this site as an attempt to give back some of what she has been given. Broken images become distracting.

Rule 62

http://www.frii.com/~buchanan/rule62/

An informative site pertaining to all things relating to twelve-step programs, including numerous resource links, self-tests, downloads & more. In keeping with the 7th Tradition of AA, all areas, including the downloads, are provided free.

Substance Abuse Resources

http://www.clark.net/pub/pwalker/
Health_and_Human_Services/Substance_Abuse/

This site provides an excellent short list of treatment resource links available online. Short descriptions are provided for each resource. Resources are listed alphabetically. The site is in-frequently updated.

part

2

Women for Sobriety, Inc.

http://www.mediapulse.com/wfs/

Women for Sobriety, Inc. (WFS) is a nonprofit organization dedicated to helping women overcome alcoholism and other addictions. The New Life program helps achieve sobriety and sustain ongoing recovery. A broad overview of the organization is provided, including special reports on the 1997 WFS Conference, WFS Group info, and the WFS bookstore.

Addiction Resource Guide

http://www.seaside.net/homepage/ovvs/1.html

Addiction Resource Guide is an online directory of inpatient and outpatient treatment facilities. The site has included information about addictions and how the layperson or professional can find the appropriate treatment options. To make navigation easier, resources are divided into appropriate categories. A brief description is provided for each resource listed.

Recovery Anonymous

http://www.mlode.com/~ra/

The author shares his personal experience of recovery. He includes information on all aspects of addictions and how these addictions interact. The inconsistent layout interferes with navigation.

Recovery Poetry Spa

http://www.geocities.com/HotSprings/Spa/1416/

This site features poetry about abuse, addictions, and recovery from them. It invites additional submissions from others. Additional links to recovery and general poetry sites are included.

National Association of Addiction Treatment Providers

http://www.naatp.org/

National Association of Addiction Treatment Providers is dedicated to raising public awareness of addiction as a treatable disease and securing adequate reimbursement for treatment programs. This site is directed toward professional development and membership education. They offer the opportunity to apply for membership or request further information. Laypersons may not benefit significantly from this site.

Volition and Addiction

http://www.geocities.com/Athens/Delphi/6797/index.html

This site focuses the problem of immediate gratification on psychological and biological variables pertaining to addiction and the exercise of will or self-determination. Outlines reactions people suffer when abstaining from addictions and alternative methods of treatment.

Illusion of Drugs

http://www.donparker.com/

Entertaining magician with an anti-drug message Don Parker, a former addict, has created a page with some information, moderate self-promotion, and lots of entertainment for the technical savvy with the latest plug-ins. A strong message is presented, but little information joins it.

BEHAVIORAL DISORDERS

ODD

http://www.conductdisorders.com

Try this website for more information on ODD and other conduct disorders.

National Center of PTSD (Post Traumatic Stress Disorder)

http://dartmouth.edu/dms/ptsd

Available on this site are research and education on PTSD, training opportunities, and information for victims, trauma survivors, clinicians, researchers, and students.

The Something Fishy Web site on Eating Disorders

http://www.something-fishy.org

This site contains updates for information, Q & A, motivations for recovery, book recommendations, chatroom connections, and treatment options.

part
2

Cyberpsych Anxiety Disorders Page

http://www.cyberpsych.org/anxdisor/anxiety.htm

This metasite has links to a variety of anxiety disorders including panic disorders, childhood phobias, and PTSD.

Anxiety Panic Internet Resources (tAPir)

http://www.algy.com/anxiety

Excellent resource for relaxation techniques, articles, diagnosis, prevention, links, and databases.

Bipolar Disorders Information Web Site

http://www.mhsource.com/bipolar

Online question and answer forum sponsored by Charles W, Bowden, M.D. and Alan Swann, M.D. the first Tuesday of each month from 10 to 11 P.M. (Eastern time). This site is operated by the Continuing Medical Education, Inc.

part

2

Dual Diagnosis

http://www.monumental.com/arcturus/dd/ddhome.htm

This resource page for treatment providers working with co-occuring disorders (MH/SA) contains NOVAADAC (Northern Region of the Virginia Association of Alcoholism and Drug Abuse Counselors) newsletter, DSM-IV Axis II personality disorders, a bookstore, and a colleagues page.

Dual Diagnosis Credentialed Listserv

To subscribe email:Listserv@maelstrom.stjohns.edu

The text of your message should read: subscribe DUALDIAG <your full name>

Dual Diagnosis Web Site

http://www.erols.com/ksciacca

Sciacca is comprehensive service development for mental illness, drug addiction and alcoholism (MIDAA). This site is designed to provide information and resources for service providers, consumers, and family members seeking assistance and education in this field.

Dual Diagnosis Online Dictionary of Mental Health

`http://www.human-nature.com/odmh/dual.html`

Sciacca hosts this Web site for co-occuring mental illness and substance disorders. Complete articles and chapters may be read and downloaded. Also included are a search engine and mailing lists.

For Today's Families (With Children and Adolescents With Brain Disorders)

`http://www.nami.org/youth/dualdigf.htm`

Fact page containing information on recovery for substance abuse and brain disorders (mental illness) as well as ADHD, depression, and bipolar disorder. Good information for families with adolescents.

PHYSICAL CONDITIONS

Teen Pregnancy Report

`http://aspe.hhs.gov/hsp/teenp/97-98rpt.htm`

Recently released online, this document, introduced in January, 1997, by the U.S. Department of Health and Human Services is the first annual report on the progress of the National Strategy to Prevent Teen Pregnancy. The report does contain some good news—teen birth rates have decreased nationally and in all states since 1991, falling twelve percent nationally and sixteen percent or more in seventeen states. The report contains statistics and analysis of teen birth and pregnancy rates, by age and race. It also details the strategies and partnerships forged by the HHS to continue this encouraging trend. Appendixes include Teenage Birth Rates in the United States, National and State Trends, 1990–96, an overview of various HHS teen pregnancy provision programs, and Teen Parent Provisions by State.

Teen Pregnancy

`http://aspe.hhs.gov/hsp/teenp/intro.htm`

The National Campaign to Prevent Teen Pregnancy has a very comprehensive site from parent brochures to resources they recommend. It may

part

2

lead you in the direction of a curriculum. There are also awareness week materials for May.

American Foundation for AIDS Research

http://www.amfar.org

The American Foundation for AIDS Research (AmFAR) is the nation's leading nonprofit organization dedicated to the support of AIDS research (both basic biomedical and clinical research), education for AIDS prevention, and sound AIDS-related public policy development.

Health On the Net Foundation

http://www.hon.ch

Health On the Net Foundation is a nonprofit organization whose mission is to build and support the international health and medical community on the Internet and World Wide Web, so that the potential benefits of this new communications medium may be realized by individuals, medical professionals, and healthcare providers. HON site includes a complete list of hospitals on the World Wide Web, Internet medical support communities (listservers, newsgroups, and FAQs), medical sites, and search engines.

HIV InSite

http://hivinsite.ucsf.edu

HIV InSite is a project of the University of California, San Francisco, AIDS Program at San Francisco General Hospital, and the UCSF Center for AIDS Prevention Studies, which are programs of the UCSF AIDS Research Institute.

JAMA HIV/AIDS Information Center

http://www.ama~assn.org/special/hiv/hivhome.htm

The JAMA HIV/AIDS Information Center is an easy-to-use, interactive collection of useful and high-quality resources for physicians, other health professionals, and the public.

Medscape

http://www.medscape.com

part
2

This is a new, free Web site for health professionals and interested consumers. Practice-oriented information is peer-reviewed and edited by thought leaders in AIDS, infectious diseases, urology, and surgery. Highly-structured articles and full-color graphics are supplemental with stored literature searches and annotated links to relevant Internet resources. From SCP Communications, Inc., one of the world's leading publishers of medical journals and medical education programs.

VIOLENCE AND TRAUMA

The Beck Specialized Treatment Assessment Inventory for Adolescents (BSTAI-A) Research Edition

Email: BeckAssociates@susquehanna-institute.com
http://www.susquehanna-institute.com

This instrument has been used by counselors, psychologists, psychiatrists, juvenile justice, and family and children service professionals, as well as school professionals in various pilots. In a relatively non-threatening and open-ended manner, this protocol asks the questions in a way that allows the interview to access such things as the experiencing of, participating in, witnessing of, or being victimized by such things as physical violence or other forms of trauma.

Victims' Rights

http://www.ojp.usdoj.gov/ovc/new/directions

This recent report from the U.S. Department of Justice (USDOJ) Office for Victims of Crime (OVC) outlines a comprehensive plan for improving the rights of and services for crime victims in the United States While making some sixty-eight recommendations for improvement, the report also notes the advances that have been made in recent years, highlighting some of the hundreds of "innovative public policy initiatives and community partnerships that are revolutionizing the treatment of crime victims in America today." Users may download the full report in ASCII or.pdf format or view individual chapters in HTML, ASCII or .pdf formats.

CHILD ABUSE

The National Victim Center/Child Abuse Bibliography

http://www.ncjrs.org/txtfiles/163390.txt

part

2

Higher Education Center Against Violence and Abuse

http://www.umn.edu/mincava

SUICIDE/DEATH/DYING

Crisis, Grief and Healing: Men and Women

http://www.webhealing.com

Suicide Facts

http://www.nimh.nih.gov/research/suifact.htm

PREVENTION SITES

National Directory of Drug and Alcoholism Treatment and Prevention Programs

http://www.health.org/search/treatdir97.htm

This site offers a database providing a 1997 listing of federal, state, local, and private providers of alcoholism, drug abuse treatment, and prevention services by city, state, territory, and zip code.

Media Campaign in Action

http://www.mediacampaign.org/index.html

National youth anti-drug campaign.

Project Know

http://www.projectknow.com/site_map.html

The Athletic Initiative Against Drugs

http://www.ondcpsports.org/scrapbook.html

Society for Prevention Research

http://www.osic.org/spr/sprhome.html

part
2

The focus of this society is broadly defined and concerned with the problems pertaining to the prevention of drug and alcohol abuse and associated social maladjustment, crime, and behavior disorders.

Project CRAFT

http://www.unm.edu/~craft

Project CRAFT, as part of the Research Division at The University of New Mexico Center on Alcoholism, Substance Abuse, and Addictions (UNM-CASAA), involves several treatment outcome studies designed to teach skills to help loved ones of resistant substance abusers convince the users to accept treatment for their drug or alcohol problems.

PREVLINE: Prevention Online at the National Clearinghouse for Alcohol and Drug Information (NCADI)

http://www.samhsa.gov

PREVLINE is the name of the NCADI's multi-faceted online information activity. NCADI services include an information services staff equipped to respond to the public's alcohol, tobacco, and illicit drug (ATID) inquiries; the distribution of free ATID materials, including fact sheets, brochures, pamphlets, posters, and video tapes from an inventory of over 1,000 items; customized annotated bibliographies from alcohol and other drug databases consisting of over 36,000 records; a Prevention Materials Database (PMD); and Federal grant announcements and application kits for prevention programs, treatment, and research funding opportunities.

part

2

National Inhalant Prevention Coalition

http://www.inhalants.org

Synergies, a nonprofit corporation founded by Harvey J. Weiss and based in Austin, Texas, established the National Inhalant Prevention Coalition (NIPC) in 1992. The NIPC grew from a state-wide prevention project in Texas called the Texas Prevention Partnership which began in 1990. NIPC is a public-private effort to promote awareness and recognition of the problem of inhalant use. NIPC is funded in part by the Robert Wood Johnson Foundation and is led by Synergies.

American Academy of Addiction Psychiatry

http://members.aol.com/addicpsych/private/
homepage.htm

The American Academy of Addiction Psychiatry was formed to promote excellence clinical practice in addiction psychiatry; educate the public to influence public policy regarding addictive illness; promote accessibility of quality treatment for all patients; provide continuing education for professionals in the field of addiction psychiatry; disseminate new information in the field of addiction psychiatry; and encourage research on the etiology, prevention, identification, and treatment of the addictions.

American Society of Addiction Medicine

http://www.asami.org

The nation's medical specialty society is dedicated to educating physicians and improving the treatment of individuals suffering from alcoholism or other addictions.

Center for Alcohol and Addiction Studies

http://www.caas.brown.edu

The Center's mission is to promote the identification, prevention, and effective treatment of alcohol and other drug use problems in our society through research, publications, education, and training.

Center for Prevention Research at the University of Kentucky

http://www.uky.edu/RGS/PreventionResearch/
welcome.html

The Center for Prevention Research at the University of Kentucky was established in October, 1987, with funding from the National Institute on Drug Abuse. It was the first such center funded by NIDA.

Growing Up Drug-Free: A Parent's Guide to Prevention

http://www.ed.gov/offices/OESE/SDFS/parents_guide

This site includes suggestions for talking with your children effectively, what to do if you think your child might be using drugs, how to teach your child about drugs, where to get information and help, and more.

part
2

The Centers for Disease Control and Prevention's (CDC) National Prevention Information Network (NPIN)

http://www.cdcnpin.org

CDC's National Prevention Information Network is designed to facilitate sharing of HIV/AIDS, STD, and TB information and resources.

National Association of State Alcohol and Drug Abuse Directors (NASADAD)

http://www.nasadad.org/prevhme1.htm

This site links to conference announcements, community anti-drug coalitions and treatment innovations and initiations.

Safe and Drug Free Schools Program

http://www.health.org/links.htm

TREATMENT STUDIES

Drug Abuse Treatment Outcome Study (DATOS)

http://www.datos.org

The Drug Abuse Treatment Outcome Study (DATOS) is NIDA's third national evaluation of treatment effectiveness. It is based on over 10,000 admissions during 1991–1993 to ninety-six community-based treatment programs in eleven large United States cities.

SUPPORT GROUPS

Eating Disorder Support Groups

http://www.hazelden.com

Overeaters Anonymous (OA) is based on the principles of AA.

Rational Recovery (RR) Support Group

http://rational.org/recovery

RR was developed by Jack and Lois Trimpey. Jack has tended to focus on alcoholism and drug addiction. Lois has written mostly about food addictions. Evolved from RET.

part
2

Smart Recovery

http://www.smartrecovery.org/

This is a self managment and recovery Web site featuring online recovery meetings Monday and Friday at 10:00 P.M. EST.

Clinical Psychology/Mental Health

MENTAL HEALTH SITES

BeckNet

http://www.susquehanna-institute.com

Professional Counselors in Private Practice Forum and Chat Room.

http://www.delphi.com/dredbeck

The forum has discussion areas on case consultation, practice management, managed care, standards and credentials, and other topics important to professional counselors in private practice. It is hoped that private practitioners and others aspiring to private practice will join in on Wednesday night chats at 9:00 P.M. ET hosted by Ed Beck and others. Watch for special topics, post your messages, and have them responded to by your colleagues. If Dr. Beck is not there, feel free to chat among yourselves. This service is completely free and a public service of the Susquehanna Institute, a multidisciplinary professional counseling service. For Further Information contact: Dr. Edward S. Beck, Director, Susquehanna Institute, 2405 Linglestown Road, Harrisburg, PA 17110–9429, (717) 545-5500(voice)/(717) 545-5858 (fax) esb1@juno.com (email)

Search Engine

http://www.cmhc.com

This search engine is devoted to mental health issues.

American Counseling Association

`http://www.counseling.org.`

This site is a must for all counselors! It contains current information on conferences, resources, books, and listservs.

Inter Psych

`http://www.shef.ac.uk/uni/projects/gpp`

SEPI

`http://www.cyberpsych.org/sepi.htm`

This site is run by the Society for the Exploration of Psychotherapy Integration

The Gestalt Therapy Page

`http://www.gestalt.org/index.htm`

American Psychoanalytic Association

`http://apsa.org`

Institute for Rational Emotive Behavior Therapy

`http://www.iret.org`

Behavior Online

`http://behavior.net`

Radical Psychology Network

`http://www.uis.edu/~radpsy`

Association for the Advancement of Gestalt Therapy

`http://www.g-g.org/aagt`

Index of Health

`http://www.chebucto.ns.ca/Health`

part
2

Psychodrama

http://csep.sunyit.edu/~joel/asgpp.html

The Focusing Institute

http://www.focusing.org

Ecopsychology, Theory, and Practice

http://www.well.com/user/suscon/esalen

Art Therapy

http://www.arttherapy.org/

Self-Psychology Page

http://www.selfpsychology.org

Personality & Consciousness

http://www.wynja.com/personality/theorists.html

Sketches of leading theorists.

Classic Theories of Child Development

http://idealist.com/children

Narrative Psychology Internet and Resource Guide

http://web.lemoyne.edu/~hevern/narpsych.html

Counselor Net—SUNY Plattsburgh

http://www.plattsburgh.edu/cnet

The Counseling Web: Counseling Psychology Programs and Resources

http://seamonkey.ed.asu.edu/~gail

The Counselor Link

http://www.counselorlink.com

Web Site for Counselor Educators and Supervisors

http://www.nevada.edu/~ces

Psych Site

http://stange.simplenet.com/psycsite/

This Web site provides psychological resources.

Psych Web for Psychology Links

http://www.gasou.edu/psychweb

Mental Health Net

http://www.cmhc.com

Mental Health Resources on the Net

http://www.cc.emory.edu/WHSCL

Counseling Licensing Exam Prep Materials

http://www.a-zuc.com/counseling.

Behavior OnLine: The Mental Health and Behavioral Science Meeting Place

http://www.behavior.net

Community Outreach Health Information System (Boston University Medical Center)

http://web.bu.edu/COHIS

Depression Central

http://www.psycom.net

part

2

National Depressive and Manic Depressive Association

http://www.ndmda.org

This site contains information and advocacy with links to support groups, patient/consumer reports, depression information, patient assistance programs, education, and diagnosis.

PsychScapes Worldwide: Connections in Mental Health

http://www.mental-health.com

Mental Health Infosource

http://www.mhsource.com

Internet Mental Health Resources

http://freenet.msp.mn.us/cgi-bin/webglimpse/home/www/root/wgsearch?query=mental+health

part 2

Your Health Daily

http://yourhealthdaily.com/live

This site offers the latest news and information on mental health from *New York Times* news syndicate.

Working with Addictive Disorders

http://www.lasalle.edu/~chapman

Internet Mental Health

http://www.mentalhealth.com

This site is an online resource for schizophrenia and other mental health information.

National Council for Community Behavioral Healthcare

http://www.nccbh.org

This site contains membership information, educational resources, a marketplace, a job bank, and public policy.

Medical and Clinical Supersites for Professionals

http://members.aol.com/texaspam/admin6.htm

Pam Pohly's Net Guide contains medical and clinical supersites. A splash page with over fifty sites includes "This Week's Hot Jobs."

American Managed Behavioral Healthcare Association

http://www.ambha.org

These online resources contain membership, links to mental health sites, and reports and studies.

Trauma and CISD Menu Page

http://eap.com.au/cisd.htm

This site is an employee assistance program for IPS located in Australia.

At Health Mental Health

http://www.athealth.com

This Web site contains a directory of professionals, newletters, professional registration, treatment centers, a resource link, books for professionals and a psychotropic resource link.

NAMI

http://www.nami.org

National Alliance for the Mentally Ill produces this site, which contains the following links: book reviews, family support, a helpline, and legal issues for the mentally ill.

Kübler-Ross: Death and Dying

http://www.doubleclickd.com/kubler.html

Resources on Death and Dying

http://www.adec.org/
http://www.adec.org/pubs/lmd/lmdltr.htm

part
2

Bereavement CD

```
http://www.bouldenpub.com
Email: jboulden@bouldenpub.com
```

Publications for Children in Distress has an interactive CD for their book, *Saying Good-bye,* which is used by seventy-five percent of the hospices and twenty-five percent of the elementary schools in the United States. The CD-ROM contains the story line of the book with animation, music, and color plus exercises for processing emotions and built-in counselor support for questions children often ask about death. Available from: Dr. Jim Boulden, Publications for Children in Distress, P. O. Box 1186, Westerville, CA 96093, (916) 623-5399 FAX (916) 623-5525

Florida Mental Health Institute

```
http://hal.fmhi.usf.edu
```

Dr. Bob's Mental Health Links

```
http://uhs.bsd.uchicago.edu/~bhsiung
```

Medweb

```
http://www.cc.emory.edu/WHSCL
```

1-800-THERAPIST NETWORK

```
http://www.1-800-therapist.com
```

Kevin Grold, Ph.D. President, 1-800-THERAPIST NETWORK, the largest multidisciplinary therapist referral service. Either fax (619-481-5143), phone (619-481-1515), or Email: referral@1–800-therapist.com

Deaf Awareness

```
http://deafness.miningco.com/library/bltopic.htm
```

CyberPsychLink

```
http://www.cyber-psych.com/
```

part
2

This site includes links and information for Psychology and Behavioral Medicine. Catalogues include listservs, newsgroups, databases, libraries, and software.

MARRIAGE AND FAMILY SITES

Marriage and Family Web Site

```
http://iamfc.org
http://iamfc.org/links.htm
```

KidsPsych

```
http://www.kidspsych.org
```

Developed by the American Psychological Association (APA), KidsPsych is a new "online adventure" for children and their parents. The Shockwave-powered site contains interactive games for children ages one through nine.

Family Involvement

```
http://pfie.ed.gov
```

The new Partnerships for Family Involvement in Education (PFIE) home page, developed with *USA Today*, offers a weekly "Spotlight" on education and PFIE issues; examples of how families, schools, businesses, and community and religious organizations are improving education in their communities; and how you can get involved. A "Partner Listing" database can help you find a particular organization among the more than 4,000 PFIE member organizations nationwide.

The International Association of Marriage and Family Counselors' Network (IAMFCNET-L) Discussion List

```
http://www.iamfc.org
```

Membership in the International Association of Marriage and Family Counselors (IAMFC) is not required to be a part of the listserv, but it is encouraged. To subscribe to the IAMFCNET-L, address an email message to Listserv@listserv.kent.edu and leave the "subject" blank. The text of the message: sub iamfcnet-l <firstname lastname>. For example: sub iamfcnet-l richard watts. Send message

part
2

Sex Surrogates

http://iamfc.org/links.htm

Divorce Sites

http://www.divorcenet.com/
http://mentalhelp.net/psyhelp/chap10/chap10o.htm
http://mentalhelp.net/guide/divorce.htm
http://mentalhelp.net/articles/child7.htm
http://mentalhelp.net/guide/relation.htm

CURRENT TRENDS

Bazelon Center for Mental Health Law

http://www.bazelon.org

Based in Washington D.C., the Bazelon Center for Mental Health Law is a nonprofit legal advocacy organization for people with mental illness and mental retardation.

PsychNews Int'l

Email: Psychnews@psychologie.de
Email: Pni@badlands.nodak.edu

This site describes mental health related resources currently available, or announced, on the Internet. Submit all contributions or corrections for the Resource Update section to the PsychNews Int'l mailboxes.

Knowledge Exchange Network (KEN)

http://www.mentalhealth.org

KEN is a one-stop source of information and resources on prevention, treatment, and rehabilitation services for mental illness. KEN is a service of the Center for Mental Health Services, Substance Abuse and Mental Health Services Administration, U.S. Department of Health and Human Services. KEN offers information related to Consumers/Survivors, Managed Care, Children's Mental Health, Statistics, and upcoming conferences and events. KEN offers an online database lookup of mental health resources around the country and in your community. KEN offers an extensive catalog of free publications, many of which can be viewed at the site or downloaded via FTP. All of the publications can be ordered via an online order form.

Childhood Sexual Abuse Manual

Email: sampson1@ix.netcom.com

The New York State Office of Mental Health is making available a manual to persons working with survivors of childhood sexual abuse. The manual is entitled *Understanding and Dealing with Sexual Abuse Trauma: An Educational Group for Women* and was written by Dr. Kristina Muenzenmaier, Donald Sampson, and others.

Shamanic Healing for Abuse Survivors

http://www.loop.com/~shaman/

Shamanic healing Web site for "body, mind, and spirit" specializing in survivors of childhood abuse. This site contains links to relevant sites.

Sandplay Therapists of America

http://www.sandplayusa.org

Playrooms

http://www.playrms.com

A great starter kit and figures for sale. Phone: 1-800-667-2470

Play Therapy

http://www.amazon.com

Windows to Our Children is a wonderful resource for working with children. Violet Oaklander's model, however, is Gestalt Therapy and if you are looking specifically for ways to use Play Therapy with children, the following books are a great starting point for a non-directive approach:

- *Play Therapy*, Virginia Axline.
- *Play Therapy, The Art of Relationship*, Garry L. Landreth.
- http://www.amazon.com and type in Play Therapy.

part

2

Alzheimer Treatment and Cause

`http://www.alz.org`

Obsessive Compulsive Disorder (OCD)

`http://www.studyweb.com/mental/menocd.htm`

Psychologists' Desk Reference

`http://www.Amazon.com`

Self Improvement Online

`http://selfgrowth.com/therapy.html`

This site contains sponsor Web sites and ninety-four additional related Web sites related to therapy and counseling.

JOURNALS

Psychwatch.com Counseling Journals

`http://www.psychwatch.com/counsel_journals.htm`

This metasite links to forty counseling journals.

PSYCHOLOGY JOURNALS

American Psychiatric Association and American Psychological Association Online Journal

`http://www.journals.apa.org/prevention/`

A new online journal that is being jointly sponsored by the American Psychiatric Association and the American Psychological Association, by Martin E. P. Seligman and Donald F. Klein. It's also free and contains an email discussion list for subscribers to discuss the latest in psychological and psychiatric outcome/treatment research. Included is information on the Planetree model of patient-centered health care that is emerging as an alternative to traditional managed care. Interestingly, Planetree has not yet filtered down to mental health and counseling but is now represented by fifteen hospitals in the United Steates, as well as in Norway and England.

Psycoloquy

```
http://www.w3.org/hypertext/DataSources/bySubject/
Psychology/Psycoloquy.html
```

Theory and Psychology Journal

```
http://www.psych.ucalgary.ca/thpsyc/thpsyc.html
```

Journal of Cognitive Rehabilitation

```
http://www.inetdirect.net/nsp
```

Pre- and Perinatal Psychology Journal

```
http://www.birthpsychology.com/journal/index.html
```

The Sport Psychologist

```
http://www.humankinetics.com/
```

Behavioral Healthcare Tomorrow Journal

```
http://www.centralink.com/journal
```

Bulletin of the Menninger Clinic

```
http://www.guilford.com/periodicals/jnme.htm
```

Journal of Applied Psychology

```
http://www.apa.org:80/journals/apl.html
```

Journal of Psychology and Human Sexuality

```
http://web.spectra.net/cgi-bin/haworth/
j-title_search?SearchTitle=
```

Journal of Social and Clinical Psychology

```
http://www.guilford.com/periodicals/jnsc.htm
```

Genetic, Social, and General Psychology Monographs

```
http://www.heldref.org/html/body_mono.html
```

part

2

International Bulletin of Political Psychology

http://www.pr.erau.edu/~security/index.html

Journal of Applied Behavioral Research

http://www.vhwinston.com/jabr

Journal of Applied Social Psychology

http://www.vhwinston.com/jasp

Journal of Comparative Psychology

http://www.apa.org:80/journals/com.html

Journal of Gerontology: Psychological Sciences

http://gsa.iog.wayne.edu/journals/psychological.html

American Psychologist

http://www.apa.org/journals/amp.html

ReVision: A Journal of Consciousness and Transformation

http://www.heldref.org/html/body_rev.html

Journal of Humanistic Psychology

http://www.sagepub.co.uk/journals/details/j0118.html

Cultural Diversity and Ethnic Minority Psychology

http://www.apa.org/journals/cdp.html

Journal for Specialists in Group Work

http://www.counseling.org/journals/jsgwinfo.htm

Journal of Mind and Behavior

http://kramer.ume.maine.edu/%7Ejmb/welcome.html

American Journal of Community Psychology

http://www.plenum.com/title.cgi?2011

APA Monitor

http://www.apa.org/monitor

Development and Psychopathology

http://www.cup.org/Journals/JNLSCAT/dpp.html

Developmental Review

http://www.apnet.com/www/journal/dr.htm

Child and Family Behavior Therapy

http://web.spectra.net/cgi-bin/haworth/
j-title_search?SearchTitle=

Child Abuse and Neglect

http://www.elsevier.nl/locate/chiabuneg

Journal of Divorce and Remarriage

http://web.spectra.net/cgi-bin/haworth/
j-title_search?SearchTitle=

Counseling and Values

http://www.counseling.org/journals/cvjinfo.htm

CTOnline

http://www.counseling.org/ctonline

Prevention and Treatment

http://journals.apa.org/prevention

part
2

ACAeNews

```
Email: enews@COUNSELING.ORG
```

Journal of Redecision Therapy

```
http://www.themetro.com/redecision
```

SOCIAL PSYCHOLOGY JOURNALS

Journal of Applied Social Psychology

```
http://www.vhwinston.com/jasp
```

American Journal of Sociology

```
http://www.journals.uchicago.edu/AJS/home.html
```

Social Psychology Quarterly

```
http://www.u.arizona.edu/~spq
```

European Journal of Social Psychology

```
http://www.interscience.wiley.com/jpages/0046-2772
```

Journal of Personality and Social Psychology

```
http://www.apa.org:80/journals/psp.html
```

Current Research in Social Psychology

```
http://www.uiowa.edu/~grpproc/crisp/crisp.html
```

Asian Journal of Social Psychology

```
http://www.blackwellpublishers.co.uk/asp/
journal.asp?ref=13672223
```

Sociological Abstracts

```
http://www.socabs.org
```

Journal of Transactional Social Psychology

http://www.bravenewweb.com/jtsp/index.html

Ethnic and Racial Studies

http://journals.routledge.com/ers.html

Social Development

http://www.blackwellpublishers.co.uk/asp/
journal.asp?ref=0961205X

Social Cognition

http://www.guifford.com/periodicals/jnco.htm

Canadian Journal of Community Mental Health Review

http://info.wlu.ca/~wwwpress/jrls/cjcmh.htm

Crisis (Journal of Crisis Intervention and Suicide Prevention)

http://www.hhpub.com/journals/crisis/index.html

Journal of Psychoeducational Assessment (JPA)

http://www.psychoeducational.com

Evidenced-Based Mental Health

http://www.bmjpg.com/data/ebmh.htm

Aging and Mental Health

http://www.carfax.co.uk/amh-ad.htm

American Indian and Alaska Native Mental Health

http://www.press.uchicago.edu/cgi-
bin/hfs.cgi/66/colorado/aian.ctl

part

2

Counseling and Values

`http://www.counseling.org/journals/cvjinfo.htm`

Journal of Mental Health

`http://www.carfax.co.uk/jmh-ad.htm`

Documentation

Your Citation for Exemplary Research

There's another detail left for us to handle—the formal citing of electronic sources in academic papers. The very factor that makes research on the Internet exciting is the same factor that makes referencing these sources challenging: their dynamic nature. A journal article exists, either in print or on microfilm, virtually forever. A document on the Internet can come, go, and change without warning. Because the purpose of citing sources is to allow another scholar to retrace your argument, a good citation allows a reader to obtain information from your primary sources, to the extent possible. This means you need to include not only information on when a source was posted on the Internet (if available) but also when you obtained the information.

The two arbiters of form for academic and scholarly writing are the Modern Language Association (MLA) and the American Psychological Association (APA); both organizations have established styles for citing electronic publications.

MLA Style

In the fifth edition of the *MLA Handbook for Writers of Research Papers,* the MLA recommends the following formats:

■ **URLs:** URLs are enclosed in angle brackets (<>) and contain the access mode identifier, the formal name for such indicators as "http" or "ftp." If a URL must be split across two lines, break it only after a slash (/). Never introduce a hyphen at the end of the first line. The

URL should include all the parts necessary to identify uniquely the file/document being cited.

```
<http://www.csun.edu/~rtvfdept/home/index.html>
```

■ **An online scholarly project or reference database:** A complete online reference contains the title of the project or database (underlined); the name of the editor of the project or database (if given); electronic publication information, including version number (if relevant and if not part of the title), date of electronic publication or latest update, and name of any sponsoring institution or organization; date of access; and electronic address.

```
The Perseus Project. Ed. Gregory R. Crane.
    Mar. 1997. Department of Classics, Tufts Univer-
    sity. 15 June 1998 <http://www.perseus.tufts.edu/>.
```

If you cannot find some of the information, then include the information that is available. The MLA also recommends that you print or download electronic documents, freezing them in time for future reference.

part
2

■ **A document within a scholarly project or reference database:** It is much more common to use only a portion of a scholarly project or database. To cite an essay, poem, or other short work, begin this citation with the name of the author and the title of the work (in quotation marks). Then, include all the information used when citing a complete online scholarly project or reference database, however, make sure you use the URL of the specific work and not the address of the general site.

```
Cuthberg, Lori. "Moonwalk: Earthlings' Finest Hour."
    Discovery Channel Online. 1999. Discovery
    Channel. 25 Nov. 1999 <http://www.discovery.com/
    indep/newsfeatures/moonwa lk/challenge.html>.
```

■ **A professional or personal site:** Include the name of the person creating the site (reversed), followed by a period, the title of the site (underlined), or, if there is no title, a description such as Home page (such a description is neither placed in quotes nor underlined). Then, specify the name of any school, organization, or other institution affiliated with the site and follow it with your date of access and the URL of the page.

O'Connor, Tom. <u>Megalinks in Criminal Justice</u>. North
    Carolina Wesleyan College. 4 Jan. 2000
    <http://faculty.ncwc.edu/toconnor/>.

Some electronic references are truly unique to the online domain. These include email, newsgroup postings, MUDs (multiuser domains) or MOOs (multiuser domains, object-oriented), and IRCs (Internet Relay Chats).

Email In citing email messages, begin with the writer's name (reversed) followed by a period, then the title of the message (if any) in quotations as it appears in the subject line. Next comes a description of the message, typically "Email to," and the recipient (e.g., "the author"), and finally the date of the message.

Davis, Jeffrey. "Web Writing Resources." Email to
    Nora Davis. 3 Jan. 2000.

Sommers, Laurice. "Re: College Admissions Practices."
    Email to the author. 12 Dec. 1999.

List Servers and Newsgroups In citing these references, begin with the author's name (reversed) followed by a period. Next include the title of the document (in quotes) from the subject line, followed by the words "Online posting" (not in quotes). Follow this with the date of posting. For list servers, include the date of access, the name of the list (if known), and the online address of the list's moderator or administrator. For newsgroups, follow "Online posting" with the date of posting, the date of access, and the name of the newsgroup, prefixed with news: and enclosed in angle brackets.

Applebaum, Dale. "Educational Variables." Online
    posting. 29 Jan. 1998. Higher Education
    Discussion Group. 30 January 1993
    <jlucidoj@unc.edu>.

Gostl, Jack. "Re: Mr. Levitan." Online posting.
    13 June 1997. 20 June 1997
    <news:alt.edu.bronxscience>.

MUDs, MOOs, and IRCs Citations for these online sources take the form of the name of the speaker(s) followed by a period. Then comes the description and date of the event, the forum in which the communication took place, the date of access, and the online address prefixed by "telnet//".

```
Guest. Personal interview. 24 December 1999.
    LinguaMOO. 24 December 1999 <telnet://du.edu:8888>.
```

For more information on MLA documentation style, check out their Web site at http://www.mla.org/set_stl.htm

APA Style

The *Publication Manual of the American Psychological Association* (4th ed.) is fairly dated in its handling of online sources, having been published before the rise of the WWW and the generally recognized format for URLs. The format that follows is based on the APA manual, with modifications proposed by Russ Dewey <www.psychwww.com/ resource/apacrib.htm>. It's important to remember that, unlike the MLA, the APA does not include temporary or transient sources (e.g., letters, phone calls, etc.) in its "References" page, preferring to handle them in in-text citations exclusively. This rule holds for electronic sources as well: email, MOOs/MUDs, list server postings, etc., are not included in the "References" page, merely cited in text, for example, "But Wilson has rescinded his earlier support for these policies" (Charles Wilson, personal email to the author, 20 November 1996). But also note that many list server and Usenet groups and MOOs actually archive their correspondences, so that there is a permanent site (usually a Gopher or FTP server) where those documents reside. In that case, you would want to find the archive and cite it as an unchanging source. Strictly speaking, according to the APA manual, a file from an FTP site should be referenced as follows:

```
Deutsch, P. (1991). "Archie-An electronic directory
    service for the Internet" [Online]. Available
    FTP: ftp.sura.net Directory: pub/archie/docs
    File: whatis.archie.
```

However, the increasing familiarity of Net users with the convention of a URL makes the prose description of how to find a file <"Available FTP: ftp.sura.net Directory: pub/archie/docs File: whatis.archie"> unnecessary. Simply specifying the URL should be enough.

So, with such a modification of the APA format, citations from the standard Internet sources would appear as follows.

FTP (File Transfer Protocol) Sites To cite files available for downloading via FTP, give the author's name (if known), the publication date (if available and if different from the date accessed), the full title of the paper (capitalizing only the first word and proper nouns), the address of the FTP site along with the full path necessary to access the file, and the date of access.

Deutsch, P. (1991) "Archie-An electronic directory service for the Internet." [Online]. Available: ftp://ftp.sura.net/pub/archie/docs/whatis.archie.

WWW Sites (World Wide Web) To cite files available for viewing or downloading via the World Wide Web, give the author's name (if known), the year of publication (if known and if different from the date accessed), the full title of the article, and the title of the complete work (if applicable) in italics. Include any additional information (such as versions, editions, or revisions) in parentheses immediately following the title. Include the full URL (the http address) and the date of visit.

Burka, L. P. (1993). A hypertext history of multiuser dungeons. <u>MUDdex</u>. http://www.utopia.com/talent/lpb/muddex/essay/ (13 Jan. 1997).

Tilton, J. (1995). Composing good HTML (Vers. 2.0.6). http://www.cs.cmu.edu/~tilt/cgh/ (1 Dec. 1996).

Telnet Sites List the author's name or alias (if known), the date of publication (if available and if different from the date accessed), the title of the article, the title of the full work (if applicable) or the name of the Telnet site in italics, and the complete Telnet address, followed by a comma and directions to access the publication (if applicable). Last, give the date of visit in parentheses.

Dava (#472). (1995, 3 November). A deadline. *General (#554). <u>Internet Public Library</u>. telnet://ipl.sils.umich.edu:8888, @peek 25 on #554 (9 Aug. 1996).

Help. <u>Internet public library</u>. telnet://ipl.org:8888/, help (1 Dec. 1996).

Synchronous Communications (MOOs, MUDs, IRC, etc.) Give the name of the speaker(s), the complete date of the conversation being referenced in parentheses (if different from the date accessed), and the title of the session (if applicable). Next, list the title of the site in italics, the protocol and address (if applicable), and any directions necessary to access the work. If there is additional information such as archive addresses or file numbers (if applicable), list the word "Available," a colon, and the archival information. Last, list the date of access, enclosed in parentheses. Personal interviews do not need to be listed in the References, but do need to be included in parenthetic references in the text (see the APA *Publication Manual*).

```
Basic IRC commands. irc undernet.org, /help (13 Jan.
    1996).

Cross, J. (1996, February 27). Netoric's Tuesday
    cafe: Why use MUDs in the writing classroom?
    MediaMoo. telenet://purple-crayon.media.mit.edu:
    8888, @go Tuesday. Available: ftp://daedalus.com/
    pub/ACW/NETORIC/catalog.96a (tc 022796.log).
    (1 Mar. 1996).
```

Gopher Sites List the author's name (if applicable), the year of publication (if known and if different from the date accessed), the title of the file or paper, and the title of the complete work (if applicable). Include any print publication information (if available) followed by the protocol (i.e., gopher://) and the path necessary to access the file. List the date that the file was accessed in parentheses immediately following the path.

```
Massachusetts Higher Education Coordinating
    Council. (1994) [Online]. Using coordination
    and collaboration to address change. Available:
    gopher://gopher.mass.edu:170/00gopher_root%3A%5B_
    hecc%5D_plan.
```

Email, Listservs, and Newsgroups Give the author's name (if known), the date of the correspondence in parentheses (if known and if different from the date accessed), the subject line from the posting, and the name of the list (if known) in italics. Next, list the address of the listserv or newsgroup. Include any archival information after the address, listing the word "Available" and a colon and the protocol and address of the archive. Last, give the date accessed enclosed in parentheses. Do not include personal email in the list of References. See the APA *Publication Manual* for information on in-text citations.

```
Bruckman, A. S. MOOSE crossing proposal.
    mediamoo@media.mit.edu (20 Dec. 1994).
```

part

2

```
Heilke, J. (1996, May 3). Re: Webfolios. acw-l@ttacs.
ttu.edu. Available: http://www.ttu.edu/lists/acw-l/
    9605 (31 Dec. 1996).
```

```
Laws, R. UMI thesis publication. alt.education.
    distance (3 Jan. 1996).
```

Other authors and educators have proposed similar extensions to the APA style, too. You can find URLs to these pages at

`http://www.psychwww.com/resource/apacrib.htm`

and

`http://www.nouveaux.com/guides.htm`

Another frequently-referenced set of extensions is available at

`http://www.uvm.edu/~ncrane/estyles/apa.htm`

Remember, "frequently-referenced" does not equate to "correct" or even "desirable." Check with your professor to see if your course or school has a preference for an extended APA style.

Glossary

Your Own Private Glossary

The Glossary in this book contains reference terms you'll find useful as you get started on the Internet. After a while, however, you'll find yourself running across abbreviations, acronyms, and buzzwords whose definitions will make more sense to you once you're no longer a novice (or "newbie"). That's the time to build a glossary of your own. For now, the 2DNet Webopædia gives you a place to start.

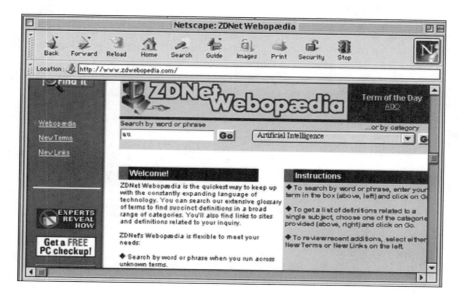

alias
A simple email address that can be used in place of a more complex one.

AVI
Audio Video Interleave. A video compression standard developed for use with Microsoft Windows. Video clips on the World Wide Web are usually available in both AVI and QuickTime formats.

bandwidth
Internet parlance for capacity to carry or transfer information such as email and Web pages.

BBS
Bulletin Board System. A dial-up computer service that allows users to post messages and download files. Some BBSs are connected to and provide access to the Internet, but many are self-contained.

browser
The computer program that lets you view the contents of Web sites.

client
A program that runs on your personal computer and supplies you with Internet services, such as getting your mail.

cyberspace
The whole universe of information that is available from computer networks. The term was coined by science fiction writer William Gibson in his novel *Neuromancer,* published in 1984.

DNS
See **domain name server.**

domain
A group of computers administered as a single unit, typically belonging to a single organization such as a university or corporation.

domain name
A name that identifies one or more computers belonging to a single domain. For example, "apple.com".

domain name server
A computer that converts domain names into the numeric addresses used on the Internet.

download
Copying a file from another computer to your computer over the Internet.

email
Electronic mail.

emoticon
A guide to the writer's feelings, represented by typed characters, such as the Smiley :-). Helps readers understand the emotions underlying a written message.

FAQ
Frequently Asked Questions

flame
A rude or derogatory message directed as a personal attack against an individual or group.

flame war
An exchange of flames (see above).

FTP
File Transfer Protocol, a method of moving files from one computer to another over the Internet.

home page
A page on the World Wide Web that acts as a starting point for information about a person or organization.

hypertext
Text that contains embedded *links* to other pages of text. Hypertext enables the reader to navigate between pages of related information by following links in the text.

LAN:
Local Area Network. A computer network that is located in a concentrated area, such as offices within a building.

link
A reference to a location on the Web that is embedded in the text of the Web page. Links are usually highlighted with a different color or underline to make them easily visible.

list server
Strictly speaking, a computer program that administers electronic mailing lists, but also used to denote such lists or discussion groups, as in "the writer's list server."

lurker
A passive reader of an Internet *newsgroup*. A lurker reads messages, but does not participate in the discussion by posting or responding to messages.

mailing list
A subject-specific automated e-mail system. Users subscribe and receive e-mail from other users about the subject of the list.

modem
A device for connecting two computers over a telephone line.

newbie
A new user of the Internet.

newsgroup
A discussion forum in which all participants can read all messages and public replies between the participants.

pages
All the text, graphics, pictures, and so forth, denoted by a single URL beginning with the identifier "http://".

plug-in
A third-party software program that will lend a web browser (Netscape, Internet Explorer, etc.) additional features.

quoted
Text in an email message or newsgroup posting that has been set off by the use of vertical bars or > characters in the left-hand margin.

search engine
A computer program that will locate Web sites or files based on specified criteria.

secure
A Web page whose contents are encrypted when sending or receiving information.

server
A computer program that moves information on request, such as a Web server that sends pages to your browser.

Smiley
See **emoticon.**

snail mail
Mail sent the old fashioned way: Write a letter, put it in an envelope, stick on a stamp, and drop it in the mailbox.

spam
Spam is to the Internet as unsolicited junk mail is to the postal system.

URL
Uniform Resource Locator: The notation for specifying addresses on the World Wide Web (e.g. http://www.abacon.com or ftp://ftp.abacon.com).

Usenet
The section of the Internet devoted to *newsgroups.*

Web browser
A program used to navigate and access information on the World Wide Web. Web browsers convert html coding into a display of pictures, sound, and words.

Web site
A collection of World Wide Web pages, usually consisting of a home page and several other linked pages.